Practical Candle Magic

Leo Vinci

Illustrations by Roger L. Fitzpatrick

CORONET

An imprint of Hodder & Stoughton
An Hachette UK company

1

A CIP catalogue record for this title is available from the British Library

Paperback ISBN 978 1 473 60636 4
Ebook ISBN 9781473606357

Printed and bound by Clays Ltd, St Ives plc

Hodder & Stoughton policy is to use papers that are natural, renewable and recyclable products and made from wood grown in sustainable forests. The logging and manufacturing processes are expected to conform to the environmental regulations of the country of origin.

Hodder & Stoughton Ltd
Carmelite House
50 Victoria Embankment
London EC4Y 0DZ

www.hodder.co.uk

CONTENTS

'It is better to light one candle than curse the darkness.'

Dedicated with love and affection
to my mother, Mona Vincent,
and Pat Arthy

INTRODUCTION

The candle (the root word appears in the Latin verb *candere*, 'to shine') forms the subject of this book. The use of ritual candles in one form or another has been with mankind for centuries, and so throughout this book the reader will find, as well as the various methods of burning candles for ritual purposes, some reference to their religious usage, history, and folklore, together with many of the myths and legends associated with them. The main subject of the work, however, is candle ritual and its method of performance.

Most people have at some time or other practised candle magic, perhaps without even realizing it. Remember your birthday cake with its candles? One for each year of your life? You were told to close your eyes, concentrate hard and make a wish, and then with a deep breath blow them all out. That was your first candle ritual. Although the history of the candle could fill many volumes, we shall only touch upon the subject briefly here.

Lamps *(lucernæ)* were in early use among the Greeks and Romans, as among the Eastern peoples. Much earlier devices for lighting, such as tapers, torches, and candles, of various materials and manufacture, have been found, especially among the poor. Primitive lights were readily available from splinters of pine and other resiniferous woods. These and other combustible materials, steeped in animal fat, oil, or tallow and fastened together with bark strips, were used as torches. Torch cases of clay and metal filled with suitable materials produced a bright, steady flame. None of these proved to have the convenience for ready use of the primitive candle, which consisted of a wick of oakum, or the dried pith of reeds and rushes, which had been steeped in wax or tallow. Furthermore, molding and shaping could produce artistic effects which probably helped to establish them firmly as a religious symbol.

The translation of candles into the early Christian faith, as with incense, was not an easy one. Many powerful voices were raised against their use and inclusion. There was strong antagonism towards these 'heathen customs,' and the 'corrupting effects' they were considered to have on the new dispensation. Tertullian (a.d. 200) came out strongly against their use, and Lanctantius (a.d. 300) proclaimed the folly of heathen worship regarding lights: 'They kindle lights to Him as though He were in darkness; if they would contemplate that heavenly light we call the Sun, they would at once perceive how God had no need of their candles. . . .'

Fortunately, these protests proved futile against the full-tide of 'heathen customs' which began to enter the church at this time, and from the fourth century onwards the practice of using candles was not only firmly established but held in high honour. Everywhere in worship, and especially on high occasions, we find candles being used, and holding a central position in processions, baptisms, marriages, and funerals. They stand on the altar; are placed before images and on shrines; and are used as votive offerings to God and the saints, or with prayer and invocation for recovery from sickness and requests for many other benefits. There are few ceremonies in which their use is not observed. Candles, when blessed, were thought to be a sure protection, a shield against thunder and lightning, protection against the blighting of crops and fields, the disease of cattle, and all manner of evils, in particular the wiles and snares of Satan. It was decreed that candles should be made solely of wax, in particular the wax of the bee, and not of tallow or other substances. 'The fragrant wax, the labour of the bee which dies when its work is accomplished, has a mystical significance. It has drawn from the best juice of plants, and has the highest natural worth as material offerings.' Tradition holds that bees originated in Paradise.

Candlemas

Though it may not prove to be its original name, Candlemas is the old English name for the Festival of the Blessed Virgin Mary on 2 February, the Venerable Bede recording the custom in the early part of the eighth century. 'La Canelière' in old France, 'Candelara' in Italy, 'Kendelmass' among the Danes and 'Lichtmesse' or 'Missa Luminum' among the Germans, all celebrate the use of the candle in this important rite. Its name refers to the actual custom of carrying lighted candles, torches, and tapers in solemn procession on this day. The 'Blessing of the New Fire,' which must, according to Mozarabic Rites, be newly struck out of flint, may perhaps link the Festival of Candlemas with the rites of Celtic heathendom.

The Celtic year began with Samhain on 1 November and the lighting of the Samhain Fires. We still keep this day as All Saint's Day or Hallowe'en. February 1st, called Brigantia, Imbolc, or Oimelc, is the first day of Spring. Candlemas (discussed later) took the place of Brigantia in the Christian calendar, but since it could not be made to match exactly, fell on 2 February. An old Scottish proverb tells us:

If Candlemass Day be dry and fair,
Then half o' winters come and mair;
If Candlemass Day be wet and foul,
Then half o' winters gone at Yule.

May 1st marked the beginning of summer with the kindling of the Beltain, Baal, or Bel Fires, the 'need fires,' and the Church decided this day should be given over to the Apostles. The fourth and last of these great festivals was 1 August, Lammas, a feast day of the Sun god Lugh, the Lughnasad Fair or Lammas Day. There are still Lammas Fairs in some country towns, and the Church takes this day to honour St. Peter.

As these occasions were all marked with fires it is not difficult to connect the 'Blessing of the Fire' with the great rites associated with them. The Scots celebrated Candle-mass Bleeze or Blaze, in honour of the old goddess Brigit, whose later Christian counterpart became St. Bride or St. Brigit. Brigit was the daughter of the powerful tribal God, the Dagda, and her feast day, La Feill Bhride, fell on 1 February. She is, in keeping with many goddesses, often portrayed in Celtic art, in Roman Gaul and Britain, as a group of three, as one of three sisters, or as a triple goddess. Even the Christian Brigit has a great deal in common with her pre-Christian counterpart. At Kildare a sacred fire was kept permanently burning at her shrine, tended by nine-teen nuns in turn, and on the twentieth day by St. Brigit herself. No man was permitted to breath on the sacred flame or come anywhere near it. In outline this resembles many of the pagan cults which were exclusive to one sex or the other. In Scotland she was known as the 'Virgin Mary's Midwife' and in this role she has often proved more pop-ular than the Virgin herself. She is invoked in matters of childbirth, particularly by the midwife while in attendance on the expectant mother. If it was thought she had been displeased, a sacrifice was offered to her. A cockerel was buried alive at a point where three streams or rivers met, in recognition of her threefold nature. The people concerned with the sacrifice burnt incense on their hearth, hardly a Christian custom.

On the eve of Candlemas in Scotland, a bed was made of corn and hay and placed near the door. When it was ready, one of the women went to the door and called out three times: 'Brigit, Brigit, come in, thy bed is ready.' One or more candles were left burning near it all night. A variation of this occurs in *Description of the Western Isles* (1860): 'The mistress and the servants of each family take a sheaf of oats and dress it up in women's apparel, put it in a large basket, and lay a wooden club by it. This they call a Briid's Bed; and then the mistress and servants cry three times, "Briid is come, Briid is welcome." This they do just before going to bed. When they rise in the morning they look among the ashes, expecting to see the impression of Briid's club there; which if they do, they reckon it a true presage of a good crop and prosperous year, and the contrary they take as an ill-omen.' This implies that on this occasion, 'Briid's Bed' is actually burnt. This has obvious connections with the Persephone cult and the revival of vegetation in spring, the candles representing the coming of the light that dispels the darkness and breaks winter's deathlike grip upon the land.

In a proclamation of Henry VIII's dated 26 February, 1530, 'concernying Rites and ceremonies to be used in due fourme in the Churche of England,' we have the following: 'On Candlemas Daye it shall be declared, that the bearynge of candels is done in the memorie of Christe the spirituall lyghte whom Simeon dyd prophecye as it is redde in the Church that daye.' In the Church of Rome it was the custom on this day to consecrate and bless all the candles that would be burnt in the churches during the coming year. At Candlemas, the Bacchanalian rite of the King or Lord of Misrule came to an end.

We see here the great wisdom of the early Church Fathers in putting their kindling upon the still warm embers of the fires they were in the process of trying to stamp out, on a hearth already established by use and generally accepted. Many early churches were likewise erected on the sites or ruins of earlier temples. The site was acceptable to the 'converts' as it was already consecrated and holy in their eyes.

It is obvious that fires were then, as now, a form of ritual purification. The whole month of February has been, from time immemorial, a month of purification. February 15th was a 'red letter day' for the women of Rome. It was in honour of Faunus, who was worshipped under the name of Lupercus in the Lupercal, a grotto in the Palatine Mount where it was said the she-wolf fed Romulus and Remus. The object of the festival was, through expiation and purification, to give new life and fruitfulness to the fields, flocks, and people. After the sacrificial feast, the Luperci or 'wolf-warders,' crowned and naked except for an apron of goatskin, ran round the ancient city on the Palatine with thongs cut from the skin of the sacrificed goats in their hands. Women used to place themselves in their path to receive blows from the thongs to charm against barrenness. The thongs were called *februa,* from the verb *februare,* 'to purify'; the day, *dies februatus,* 'the day of purification;' and the whole month, *februarius,* 'the month of purification.' The festival was observed until A.D. 494, in which year Bishop Gelasius I changed it into the Feast of Purification, 'as a check to the heathen Festival of Lupercalia.' The transference of the Festival from the 15th to the 2nd was due to the institution of the Festival of Christmas on 25 December. In A.D. 386, Chrysostom refers to the Festival of Christmas having been introduced into Antioch about A.D. 375. This is a festival of the Latin Church, and forty days of purification led to the institution of the Festival of the Presentation on 2 February.

It was certainly no accident that Candlemas Day was called in the North of England 'the Wives Feast Day.' It was sheer inspiration for the Church to consecrate the pagan February Festival in honour of the Virgin, called in the English Prayer Book 'The Purification of St. Mary the Virgin.' It commemorates the Purification of Mary when she took the infant Jesus to the Temple, where it was disclosed 'that He would grow up a light to lighten the Gentiles.' As with the Festival of Lupercalia, the theme is one of 'purification,' and the custom of Jewish mothers presenting themselves at the Temple for purification after childbirth was translated into the Christian faith as 'churching' or 'the Churching of Women.' The fortieth day was appointed for this purpose.

In a proclamation dated 16 November 1530, Henry VIII enjoined to be retained among many 'laudable ceremonies and rytes' the following: 'ceremonies used at the purification of women delivered of chylde, and offerynge of theyr crysomes.' A mother who entered a house before she was churched was considered a bearer of ill luck to the house she entered. The possible origin of this was the pre-Christian superstition that after childbirth a woman was open to the influences of the fairy world and its occupants. Irish folklore informs us that the bad luck associated with going out and about before churching could be averted by putting a little thatch, or a small piece of slate, taken from the roof of the home, on the crown of a new bonnet. In doing this, the woman was, to all intents and purposes, under her own roof and the bad luck was nullified. Meeting a man first after churching signified that the next child would be a male, meeting a woman, a girl.

The 'teending,' or lighting of the Christmas Log with the Christmas Brand laid up from Candlemas, is another echo of the sanctity of the Sacred Fire. The old idea of the continuity of the Sacred Fire and Light is shown in the burning of the Christmas Brand and its preservation till the coming Christmas:

Kindle the Christmas brand, and then
Till sunne-set let it burn;
Which quencht, then lay it up agen,
Till Christmas next returne.

Part must be kept wherewith to teend
The Christmas Log next yeare;
And where 'tis safely kept, the Fiend,
Can do no mischiefe (there).

These customs and rites show the continuity in folklore and religion of the earliest religious ideas: 'Light is a great blessing, and as great as food, for which we give thanks: and those that think this superstitious neither know superstition nor themselves.'

The calendars and service books of the church throw light on the threefold character of the Festival – as Feast of our Lord, a Feast of the Blessed Virgin Mary, and a Feast of Lights, and it is for these reasons that I have spent some little time on the Festival of Candlemas with the purpose of showing that, from pre-Christian times and through the various religious philosophies, ritual candles have a very long history upon which the reader can build his present-day efforts.

Former Uses of Candles

It is often held that if a candle flame burns blue or dimly there is a ghost or spirit in the house or nearby. In Germany, a candlewick that divides and splits the flame foretells a death in the house. A candle giving forth a spark into the air meant a letter arriving soon for the one sitting opposite or nearest. There were three main occasions on which candles were lit. At birth, they ensured that evil spirits would be kept away from the infant, and in Rome this put the child under the personal protection of the Goddess Vesta. At marriage, they prevented the 'Evil Eye' from blighting the future of the bridal couple, while candles lit at death were a safeguard, for no demon would then dare to attempt to steal the soul of the deceased. 'Candle auctions' were very common in the seventeenth and eighteenth centuries and I believe some still exist today. A pin is placed into a candle, about one inch below the wick, bidding continues until the pin drops, and the last bid made before the pin drops is the one that is taken.

In Lancashire, famous for its witches of Pendle Forest, candles were used to keep the witches and their kind at bay, especially around the time of All Hallow's Eve. Their wiles could be prevented by burning a candle which, naturally, the witches did their best to blow out. Woe betide the victim if they succeeded. If the flame could be kept burning until just after midnight, the black art of the witches was defeated.

The candle also occurs in figures of speech. Thus when a game 'is not worth a candle,' it is implied that it was not worth the effort involved, or more precisely, that it was not worth the candles that were used to light the players. An inferior person not worth consideration is 'not fit to hold a candle to . . . ,' alluding to the 'link boys' who held candles in theatres and places of amusement before the advent of electricity. It was the custom at one time to show disapproval of either actor or play by throwing a candle upon the stage, which sometimes brought the curtains down, at times perhaps even the buildings. To dissipate one's energies, to overdo work or pleasure, so as to impair one's health, is 'to burn the candle at both ends,' a bright but short existence. 'Candleholder' today usually means a candlestick of some kind, but an earlier reference was to one who aided and abetted without actually sharing in the action or undertaking: 'I'll be a candleholder and look on.' This in turn derived from the practice of a person's holding a candle for the reader in the Catholic Church. To sanction an action or deed that was deemed wrong was 'to hold a candle to the Devil,' since candles were lit to the saints for good. According to a delightful old saying, 'Tace is Latin for a candle,' which would translate today as 'keep it under your hat.' *Tace* is Latin for 'be silent' and the candle was symbolic of light, meaning, 'do not bring it into the light, keep it dark.'

A popular phrase referring to the ceremonial act of Excommunication in the Roman Catholic Church is 'by bell, book and candle.' After pronouncing the sentence of excommunication, the cleric officiating closes the book, extinguishes the candle by throwing or stubbing it on the ground, then tolls the bell, as for one who has just died. The book symbolises the Book of Life, now closed; the candle, the soul that has been removed from the sight of God, as the flame of the candle was removed from the sight of men, while the bell tolls for his 'death.'

Candles and the Dead

Candles have long been connected with death and the dead. A 'corpse' or 'fetch' candle is one which hovers in the air, evading all attempts to get near it. According to Welsh records, such candles would disappear if you tried to come near them or stand in their way. On these occasions they would vanish and presently reappear behind the observer, steadfastly holding their course. If a little candle with a pale blue flame were seen, then the corpse either of an aborted child or some infant would follow; if a larger one, then the corpse of someone 'come of age,' while two or more candles differing in shape and size indicated several corpses of different sizes and ages. If, however, two candles came from different places and were seen to meet, two corpses would soon do likewise. Sometimes these candles would show the actual places where persons would sicken and die. Many lights were often witnessed to take the exact route a burial procession would later take. If there were to be any hold-ups on the funeral route, the candle(s) would indicate where, and the amount of time spent there, by hovering over the exact spot. Tradition tells us of the promise St. David made to the Welshmen of his territory, that none should die without the foreshadowing omen of a light travelling to his house from the churchyard to summon his soul. It was believed that the flame was the spirit of a relative come to escort the soul of the dying man or woman to its rest, and this same belief is held in Devon and Cornwall, except for the fact that if the churchyard contains no relative belonging to the dying person, no corpse candle will come to escort the soul.

Candles are usually placed around a corpse to prevent the soul of the deceased from being taken. *Scroggin's Jests* (1626) informs us that in Henry VIII's reign it was the custom to set two candles to burn over the dead, one at the head and the other at the feet. The lighting of a memorial light on the anniversary of death is also a widespread practice. A method of forecasting the future among the Jewish peoples was employed during the ten days prior to Yom Kippur or Day of Atonement, for during these ten days it was said that a man's fate was determined in heaven. A candle was placed in a sheltered place and lit, and if the candle burned down to the end, the person could anticipate a further year of life, but if the candle was extinguished he would not see the year out. Basically, this is the reason for Yom Kippur, the renewal of names in the Book of Life for one more year. They would frequently burn a candle for a whole week in a room where a person had died.

Divination by Candle

Candles have long been used to predict the weather. In *Nature's Secrets* we read: 'If the flame of a candle, or lamp, or any other fire does wave or wind itself, where there is no sensible or visible cause, expect some windy weather. When candles or lamps will not so readily kindle as at other times, it is a sign of wet weather neer at hand. When candles or lamps do sparkle and rise up with little fumes, or their wicks do swell, with things on them (like mushrums) are all signs of wet weather.'

On the 'three spirit nights' or Tair Nos Ysbrydion in Wales, women gathered in the churches of the parish to try to divine their future from the candle that each held. Divination by candle is a very old art, and the forms it took can only be given brief mention. It is often called 'lychnomancy,' from the Latin *lychnus* – a light or lamp. In candle divination, the auguries are very simple and based upon observing how the candles burn. A wavering flame, not due to draughts or winds, foreshadowed a change in circumstances. A flame rising or falling indicated potential danger. A bright tip on the wick showed an increase in success or luck, but if it faded or died, such success or luck would be short-lived. If the flame appeared to turn or spiral, beware the wiles of schemers and treacherous folk. A spluttering flame presaged disappointment not long in coming. If the flame went out altogether, there would be a loss of a serious perhaps even tragic nature. A flame burning very dimly or low directs us to hold back the enquiry or venture since there is not enough light for either the enquiry or project to prosper, or illness and lack of vitality will prove a handicap. Grease congregating around the wick of the candle is a 'winding sheet,' foretelling the death of a person in the house. Sometimes more than one candle is used, the usual number being three, frequently set in the form of a triangle. If one of these number burnt higher and brighter than the others, good fortune was on the way, whereas if all three burnt exceptionally bright it was deemed the 'Blessing of Light' and most auspicious.

The reader will have seen by now that candles and lights have played a large part in the life of mankind, a part which has not diminished. Man has venerated fire in all its forms since its discovery. It gave him heat and light in the depth of winter, cooked his food, gave him protection against wild animals and from the cold. Fire added another tool with which to master the environment in which he found himself. The most sacred of the Elements of the Order of Prometheus, it dispelled cold and darkness, and brought him life and, therefore, it was not thought unreasonable that it would also dispel evil spirits and things that 'delight and work in darkness.' As it helped man in his fight to conquer these enemies of his existence, it might perhaps even help him to conquer Death itself.

The first part of what follows will deal with the necessary preparation and items used, in addition to the basic requirements of the candles. With the various tables and information given throughout the work, it should prove relatively easy to determine the requirements for formulating your own rituals. The pattern of the rituals given is fairly obvious and should be used to assist you in creating your own, for these will have the additional power of your own personal style, efforts, and mental concentration.

Candle magic is simple in form yet can be made very beautiful by this simplicity; alternatively, it can be as elaborate as you wish to make it – personal temperament dictates the form it will take. The language is straightforward and well within the range of all according to their ability. You must not think that all you have to do is burn a few candles, light some incense, and say a few words, whereupon everything will drop into your lap for the asking. Candle ritual will *not* replace personal effort.

In most spheres of human endeavour, practice is usually the 'father of theory', in that someone does something, then someone else comes along at a later date and tries to find out how, or why, it works. While not wishing to disparage theoretical study (I value it most highly myself), progress can (at times) be hindered by too much *theory* and too little *practice*.

CANDLE MAKING

If you do not make your own candles, you can purchase them from normal retail outlets, though most arts and crafts stores will have many candles of more artistic designs and unusual shapes, such as roses, crucifixes, figures, embossed candles, etc., many of which you can utilise for your purpose. The most important consideration is undoubtedly color, as will be shown later, though the most useful color of all may prove to be white. As a later section will show, you can even color white candles to suit your requirements. There was a time when I would have strongly advised you against using candles of animal fat. Though the admonition still holds good, it is not necessary today as most candles are made of paraffin wax, vegetable oils, or beeswax. You can, therefore, buy from those generally available with confidence.

The actual size is a matter of personal choice, though in general a five- or seven-inch candle is the most practical for candle work. The candles used are divided into three main groups:

Altar Candles

Altar Candles (A/Cs) are the candles placed at the rear of the altar. Two candles are usually used and this is my personal preference, but you can use a single candle if you wish, placed at the rear of your altar in the centre. Altar Candles should always be white. Buy the tallest and most beautiful you can afford. If you can obtain and afford them, use beeswax candles, as they represent the deity or God (whatever your religion or religious philosophy) and the spiritual kingdom, which is the realm you are trying to contact and forge a link with, the Altar Candles serving as your 'bridge' with that kingdom. Occasionally you may find it said that Altar Candles are not really necessary and can be omitted, but their removal breaks the pattern of three, Altar Candles, Zodiac Candles, and Offertory Candles, the ubiquitous but sacred 'trinity' of most religions, and thus reduces it to a pattern of two and 'duality'. On the earth plane, duality is frequently the cause of many of our conflicts and troubles and is often the reason for the ritual in the first place. The Altar Candles should literally dominate the altar even when the candles are burning low. They are, more often than not, the first to be lit and the last to be extinguished for 'I am the Alpha and the Omega, the first and the last.'

Zodiac Candles

The Zodiac Candles (Z/Cs), sometimes called Astral Candles, nearly always represent the people involved in the ritual according to their birth sign (which is why I prefer the term Zodiac Candle to Astral) – consult the Tables at the end of the book for this. Zodiac Candles are used to represent the petitioner, the person or persons for whom you may be performing the ritual, people you may wish to influence, or those people who are helping, obstructing, or 'crossing' the situation for which the ritual is being performed. If you do not know that person's birth sign, use a white or yellow candle; alternatively you can use an exhausted ballpoint pen to scratch the person's name in the wax of the candle.

The white candle, regarded as neutral, is an obvious choice for an unknown person or factor. The yellow alternative sometimes perplexes students, yet the reason is relatively simple. Yellow represents the planet Mercury (a greatly misunderstood planet), and the Archangel Raphael, the 'Messenger of the Gods.' He pervades all planes and, having everyone's 'ear,' relays messages or information to where it should go if you are in any doubt. In his positive aspect, he is neutral and his force acts like 'quicksilver' (a 'shapechanger'), which is his metal. He is thus well suited to this purpose and is usually deemed helpful.

Offertory Candles

Finally, we come to the Offertory Candles (O/Cs), which represent the active principle in any situation – the forces at work, for good or ill, that you are trying to manipulate one way or the other. This is shown in the choice of color and in the positions of these candles on the altar. If they are between the petitioner and the petitioned, they may be obstructing the petitioner. If they are between the petitioner and an evil, obstructive force or person, they may well be defending him, as will be shown later. These two latter sets of candles, the Zodiac and Offertory Candles, work on the front section of the altar in front of the Altar Candles, which, for the most part, remain stationary at the rear. The form of the ritual dictates the positions and movement of these candles, which will also be explained later.

Candle Making

Early schools of occultism were adamant that the magician/occultist should try to make everything he was going to use, and there was sound reasoning for this, for by making everything yourself you are giving of your time, and your time is your life. Further, in creating these artifacts, it is necessary to concentrate, in all the stages of their manufacture, on the purpose behind their use. Your equipment becomes 'impregnated' or 'charged' with your personal vibrations or thoughtforms, which, after anointment or consecration to the force or power behind their intended use, remain personal both to that force or power and to you. Traditionally, this is why these items were not publically displayed or permitted to be touched or used by anyone else. Often they were hidden away in a safe place to prevent anyone else from handling them even inadvertently and thus contaminating them or even destroying their power.

The basic materials are as follows:

Paraffin Wax

Waxes have varying degrees of melting and working temperatures. The most useful and frequently used has a melting point of 133° – 136° F (56° – 58° C).

Stearin

This is a general name for three glycerids, formed by a combination of stearic acid and glycerine, applied chiefly to tristerin, which is the chief constituent of tallow. It is a non-toxic, non-corrosive, white, flaky substance. Stearin makes the candles opaque and the percentage (a ratio of ten percent added to the wax) usually causes the mixture to shrink a little, thus allowing the candle to be extracted from the mold more easily. Wax can be purchased with the stearin already added in the correct proportions. It should be added to, and mixed in, dissolved candle dyes before the dye is added to the wax. This helps by giving better dispersion in the wax.

Wicks (Various Sizes)

The correct choice of wick is most important and must be the right type and size for the candle according to its height and girth. If the wick is too small, it will be swamped by an excess of molten wax and may go out. Too large a wick will have insufficient fuel, and if it does not go out, may burn with a very smoky flame. Often a wick slightly smaller than required is used so that the candle will burn with a hollow centre. This can be very effective in square candles, as symbols can be put on the sides, which is most impressive as the candle burns down. This type of candle makes a very potent 'magical night-light' during hours of darkness, or in times of stress and perplexity. Making sure the wick, trimmed to about a quarter of an inch, is central in the candle is most important. Keep the wick trimmed while burning and the burning area clean. You can make your own wicks of bleached and stranded cotton soaked in boracic acid. They are, however, probably best purchased from a supplier, because you will have the benefit of advice as to the most suitable type and size of wick for your purpose.

Thermometer

A good thermometer is most important, so avoid buying cheap ones. It should have a range of up to 400° F (204° C). Do not use a medical or room thermometer as these will simply shatter. Never attempt to pick off wax from the glass, but melt it first in hot water and wipe clean.

Wax Dyes

Add a very small amount of dye to the wax at first. Remember that you can always add dye more easily than take it away. Too much dye and the candle will not be translucent. Candle dyes will stain everything in sight, especially the hands, so take great care.

Perfumes

These are oil-soluble perfumes, not spirit. Use them very sparingly until you find the strength you like. This is a matter of personal choice and cannot be specified by anyone else.

Beeswax Sheets

This is usually bought in sheets, which are made pliable by using them in a warm room. Wrapped (by rolling) around a wick of appropriate size to the candle, some 'shaping' is possible. Even unlit, these candles will gently perfume the air.

Utensils

Various pans may be used according to needs. A double- boiler is very useful. If you heat your wax over an open flame, use an asbestos mat for safety at *all* times.

Molds

There are many excellent molds on the market, available from arts and crafts stores specializing in candle supplies and materials. Improvisation, however, should be your keynote. The improvisation that can be utilised in candle molds is endless. Clay, tin-foil, pots, kitchen containers, and many other ordinary things should now be looked upon as potential molds before they are thrown away. The mold must be leakproof, and obviously you must be able to separate the mold from the candle. You will find that many items can be carefully cut in half (especially plastic containers) and rejoined with strong adhesive tape to make them leakproof. The mold can then be taken apart to get the candle out when set, and any 'join marks' on the candle taken away with a sharp knife, or a warm blade.

Wicks can be inserted afterwards. Insert a skewer or long needle while the wax is still soft, pulling the wick through the candle, and then top off with hot wax to secure. Alternatively, a hand drill can be used when the candle has set. Use a thin drill, which will have to be longer than the candle, unless you drill from both ends so as to meet in the middle. Insert your wick as before and fill up the hole with wax.

Dips

The oldest method of making candles is dipping. This has several advantages for the beginner, since neither pouring techniques nor molds are required here. Decide on the length of your candle and cut your wick accordingly, with some to spare. Use a container for the melted wax longer than the proposed candle. Tie the piece of cut wick to a stick as a handle and dip in the wax, which should have been heated to 180° – 185° F (82° – 85° C), then remove it and after about thirty seconds (by which time it should be set) repeat the whole thing. Repeat this until you have the thickness of candle you require. With a receptacle of adequate size and sufficient wax, you can hang several wicks on your stick and make several candles at the same time.

Dip-Coated Candles

You can coat white candles with colored wax, a method which can prove economical. I use two methods to coat white candles with color. The first is the usual 'dip-coating' method; the second I refer to as 'drip-coating.' Let us take a look at the dip coating method first. This, as the name implies, consists of dipping white candles in colored wax in the manner described above. The preparation is, however, a little different. On hot water, float a layer of molten wax of the color you require (temperatures as given above). Make this colored layer between two and three inches thick, but not less than two inches. You will need a container that will take the length of the candle plus the depth of the colored wax, and enough space to take both the displaced hot water and colored wax when the candle is being dipped. The candle is dipped in the same manner as above, but this time, as it is pulled out, it becomes coated with a layer of the floating, colored wax. As with the previous method, you repeat the dipping until you acquire the depth of color you want. Keeping the temperature correct is most essential, and poor results will show you when this is not so. If it is too hot you will pick up little or none of the colored wax; if too cool, the colored coating will peel or flake.

Drip-Coated Candles

I must confess that I devised and experimented with this method purely as an economy measure. One colored candle will drip-coat about twelve white candles, depending on the depth of color required. With this method, as you will see later, you have one advantage in that you can place several colors on the same candle if you wish. You will soon get the knack of putting the wax in the right place. Let us say that you wanted to make a 'Money Candle.' This is made up with a white candle as a base, with the color purple, of the planet Jupiter (for money), and yellow, which is one of the colors of the Sun (representing gold: sovereigns, etc.). To this you can add green (symbolizing Venus in Taurus for 'growth'). For stability in an affair of the heart, marriage, or a partnership, you could start by placing the dark green of the planet Saturn (positive aspect) to give stability, wisdom, and a firm foundation, and add the rose-pink of Venus in Libra representing marriage, partnership, sociability, love, and companionship, so that the Libran 'scales' (of the natural seventh house) are balanced and stable. Endless possibilities lie in simply combining the information found throughout this book.

As the name implies, this method consists of dripping colored wax onto a white candle. Start by laying several layers of newspapers on the table. You can hold your white candle by its wick, resting the base on the paper. Light a candle (or any small ends – any color) in a holder or ashtray to light your colored ones from, especially if you intend to use several colors. Drip the molten wax from the colored candle onto the white. The angle at which you hold the white candle determines whether the colored wax sets into short or long runs. Any run or interesting shape can be set by gently blowing on it. You can put a quick foundation layer of color on by turning the white candle as you drip on the color, any spaces left being filled in as the candle turns. Keep doing this until you cover the white candle to the depth of color required. This method furnishes candles of interesting textures, and no two will be exactly alike. If you want to cover the entire candle with color right up to the wick, you can 'set' it quickly by putting it in the refrigerator for a while; then hold the base and drip the colored wax around the white remaining at the wick. Often I leave the curved part of the candle, around the wick, white. Burning first, this represents the Deity, like your Altar Candles, and the positive White Force you are invoking. Let me give another example. I call this an 'Angelic' or 'Planetary Candle' as it is coated with seven bands of color, one for each day of the week and the angel that rules it.

First divide your candle into seven equal sections. The order of the colors is (from the wick to the base): Sunday/orange/Sun; Monday/white/Moon; Tuesday/red/Mars; Wednesday/yellow/Mercury; Thursday/purple/Jupiter; Friday/rose-pink or blue/Venus; Saturday/dark green/Saturn. This order assumes that you want to start on Sunday; otherwise, simply start with the appropriate day at the top. Practice has taught me that it is simpler to start from the bottom of the candle and work upwards, so that you fill in the bottom band first with dark green, then the next with rose-pink or blue; and so on until the wick is reached, with orange for the Sun. Although the 'base candle' is white, you should still drip white wax into the appropriate band for the Moon/white/Monday, to maintain a consistent texture. You will not find it difficult to drip the wax into place, and if any wax occasionally runs over the next color do not worry. To remove any offending runs (should you wish to), simply let the candle set, nick the offending run with your nail at the point where the color joins and lift it off. You light this candle each day.

In the above example you would start on Sunday, burn only the appropriate section for that day, and extinguish it properly when the candle has burnt down to the next color. Invoke the appropriate angel, which is best done in the correct planetary or angelic hour, and request his protection and blessing for that day. If you cannot manage the correct planetary hour, do it as one of the first acts for that day when it is convenient, before starting the business of the day. This further example serves to show the reasoning behind this method of 'drip coating,' and you should have no trouble in devising your own candles for other specialised uses.

2

EQUIPMENT AND
GENERAL NOTES

In choosing candlesticks you may select as you wish. There is only one consideration to be taken into account, and that is that you must include in your choice some small candlesticks or holders. In candle work you often have to place two, sometimes more, candles close to each other, and if your candleholders are too large this will prove difficult. Further, the altar can tend to become rather cluttered. This does not, of course, mean that you must only use this kind of holder, merely that it is desirable to have a few. Experience alone can tell you how many you will want for rituals you wish to perform, and if it is a standard, easily obtained item, you can add to your stock later as your needs dictate. I would suggest that you start with about six small holders, glass or crystal being excellent and proving a neutral color so that any color candle can be used with them. If you can obtain a set that has seven colors, one for each of the planets of old astrology (as per Tables), so much the better.

Your Altar Candlestick(s) should be the tallest and the most ornate, or the tallest and simplest, according to personal taste. The other candlesticks can be purchased to suit individual requirements, color and shape representing the forces, signs of the zodiac, colors, angels, and so on. For example, a pink or blue holder, perhaps shaped like a rose, would represent Venus; a purple, small, swan-shaped holder, Jupiter. Anything representing a 'solar disc' that can stand behind a candle or on which a candle may stand can represent the Sun, while something silver or mother-of-pearl, perhaps a nacre-lined shell, would be appropriate for the Moon; a flat piece of rock would stand for Saturn. Any container or surface with which a candle may be *safely* used should be checked for relevant planetary or angelic rulership to see if it can be utilised.

Dressing or Anointing Candles

The most important factor in the preparation of a candle for ritual use is the 'dressing' or, as some prefer, 'anointing,' and its importance cannot be over-stressed. Anointing makes an item sacred. By this act you positively dedicate an object, no matter what, to a single purpose, which excludes its use for any other purpose. It is no use dressing a candle of precise color to a specific purpose and then using it for another.

For the purpose of 'dressing', the candle is regarded as being divided into two equal halves. From the centre to its wick is its 'north pole,' from the centre to its base the 'south pole.' To dress your candle, take some of the anointing oil on your fingers (not too much, just enough to put a light coating on the surface of the candle) and rub it on your hands. You then rub this oil on your candle in a traditionally ritual manner as follows. From the centre to the north pole (wick) and only in this direction; from the centre to the south pole (base) in a similar manner. (Do not rub the candle oil up and down *at any time*.) Make sure that both halves are dressed with the same number of strokes: you would pick a number important to you (seven, for instance), and use it for both directions. I personally stand with the candle's north pole (wick) to the actual North Pole; and its south pole (base) to the actual South Pole (use a compass or the rising sun).

During the dressing of your candle you should have been concentrating on the purpose to which the candle is to be used; the results you desire; the people involved; that which is helping or impeding the reason for the ritual; and so on. What you are concentrating on for each candle will naturally depend upon the use to which the candle is being put. You must make your concentration as sin-gle-pointed as you are able; focus it to a burning point. Do not strain at this concentration; if necessary, do it in short periods. Just as a magnifying glass concentrates the light of the sun to white heat, you must similarly 'enflame yourself with prayer.' Thought-forms are very powerful things and with these you are said to magnetise the candle, to make the candle and you one, and to impregnate the candle with your purpose and personal vibrations. The greater the intensity, the greater will be the power stored (like a battery) in the candle and waiting for the 'circuit of force' to be completed to discharge itself in a controlled manner for the purpose you intend.

For the sake of completeness I offer an alternative form of dressing which I have been using for a number of years. It is quite simple and has proved effective in personal work. Certain rituals are performed for the purpose of 'attracting or bringing down,' while others are for 'dispelling or sending away.' When I wish to attract or 'draw down' to me, I dress the candle from its north pole (wick) to its south pole (base), straight from top to bottom without any division as before. Meanwhile, you concentrate on drawing down to you and your altar (on which the candle will eventually burn) that which you desire. To dispel or banish, you merely reverse the process by dressing the candle from south to north, this time concentrating on whatever it is you wish to dispel or banish from you and your altar. When you use this alternative system, hold your candle by the base (south) with the wick (north) pointing away from you, so that when the candle is being dressed for attraction you will be drawing the oil towards yourself (wick to base); likewise, for banishment you will be dressing your candle away from you (base to wick). Both of these are symbolical acts. If you undertake to use this second system, remember its employment is restricted to rituals of either attraction or banishment. Please remember, if you are in doubt, the traditional system is the one to use.

Candle Anointing or Dressing

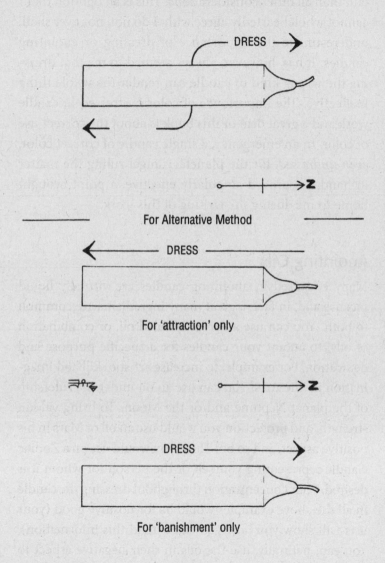

For Alternative Method

For 'attraction' only

For 'banishment' only

Figure 1

Some writers say that dressing a candle is more important than all other considerations. This is an opinion that I cannot wholeheartedly agree with. I do not, nor ever shall, underestimate the importance of dressing or anointing candles. It has, however, always seemed to me that dressing the wrong kind of candle can render the whole thing ineffective. The importance of color is stressed in candle work and a great deal of this book is about the correct use of color. In an emergency, a single candle of correct color, *even undressed,* for the planetary angel ruling the matter in hand has proved singularly effective, a point brought home to me during the writing of this work.

Anointing Oils

Many oils used in anointing candles are virtually liquid incense and, in fact, a great many ingredients are common to both. You can use a correctly ruled oil, or combination of oils, to anoint your candles for a specific purpose and dedication. For example: to increase artistic skill and imagination in 'the Arts,' you can use an oil under the rulership of the planet Neptune and/or the Moon. To bring valour, strength, and protection you would use an oil of Mars in his positive aspect, and so on. These you would use on a Zodiac Candle representing yourself or the person for whom it is desired. Your concentration throughout dressing the candle in all the above examples would be for positive good (your lists will show you how you can extend this information). You can, naturally, use the oils in their negative aspect to reinforce and enhance the negative aspects of your candles.

The use of any of these negative methods in an unjust or evil cause is *not* to be encouraged. By unjustly so doing, you may find yourself in the unenviable position of being 'judged' instead of 'judging.' The only defence you can have is a 'just' cause; but if you are in *any* doubt, you do not have one.

A good oil for general use if you cannot obtain anointing oils is olive oil (though a pure vegetable oil may be used, e.g., corn oil, sunflower oil). Olive oil is easy enough to get and is attributed to the Goddess Minerva, the Goddess of Wisdom, a very good force to invoke (you can simply invoke for 'wisdom in the matter'). Candle perfumes are an excellent alternative. These oils are easy to obtain in the appropriate perfumes which can be used for anointing and dressing.

The Altar

For an altar you can use whatever is convenient, though it should, however, be reasonably stable. It can be square, but the ideal shape for ritual candle work has proven to be oblong, as some of the rituals involve moving candles over a few days, so the more room to do this the better (coffee tables are ideal). You can cover it with an altar cloth, which should definitely be used if the 'altar' is used for other purposes, as the altar cloth acts as an 'insulator' against the mundane vibrations of its dual use, keeping the ritual area clean for ritual work. Thin material may prove most suitable; silk is best as an insulator. It could be of the color of the sign of the zodiac in which your

Sun was placed at birth, with which you have a natural affinity.

Can any statues or figures be placed on the altar? This is entirely up to you, but there is no reason why any symbol of your particular faith or religious philosophy cannot be used. The risen and crowned 'Christus Rex' is better than the crucified Christ figure (a personal opinion), as it symbolises the defeat of death rather than the sacrifice to it (as the Cathar peasants are reputed to have said, 'Would you worship the gallows on which your father had died?'). The patron saint of the country is an excellent wellspring. I find the presence of St. George in the centre of my altar to be of inestimable benefit and value. He always gives strength and dignity to whatever he is associated with, and I am unable to find words to recommend his use strongly enough to those whose patron saint he is. Though not essential, a useful recommendation is the employment of a 'balancing force,' a symbol or figure to represent the gender complementary to the person performing the ritual. As a male, I often use a female figure, mostly the lunar, Chinese 'Goddess of Mercy' – Kuan Yin: a female practitioner would, naturally, use a male figure or symbol. These symbols should be placed at the rear of the altar, in the centre, between the Altar Candles with your incense placed before it. Some place a Bible on the altar (those of Christian persuasion often using the texts for the rituals).

If possible the room should be set apart from the general run of the house, as some of the rituals involve leaving the candles to burn out naturally, and others require several days' work, which entails leaving the altar with the candles undisturbed between rituals until the following day. A room used for ritual purposes exclusively has a 'power build-up,' the value of which cannot be overestimated. Those whose circumstances prevent them from doing this will have to dismantle the altar and reassemble it the next day. If it has to be done this way the continuity will be lacking; but if it cannot be avoided, then I believe any ritual is better than none at all. The obvious precautions against fire must be observed.

Lighting and Extinguishing Candles

At first it may appear strange that it should be necessary to tell people how to light and extinguish candles, a simple enough operation, after all. First, always use matches. The action of 'striking' the match to create fire is symbolic of the Mozarabic Ritual, still used today for calling up 'new fires' by striking flint. It is often a good idea to have a supply of either wax tapers or wooden spills to transfer the light to other candles once the altar candles have been lit.

Do not snuff the candles out between your finger and thumb, but with a candle-snuffer. Modern reproductions have appeared on the market in recent years. If you cannot get one, they only involve some basic metal work, being simply a cone on the end of a handle. In the absence of this, cup the candle behind the flame with your hand and blow it out.

You can make excellent individual snuffers from kitchen foil. They are simply small cones, or 'dunce's caps,' of foil which are placed on each candle in order. I use a saucer as a template, about five or six inches in diameter. Lay the foil on some paper, and lightly mark around the rim of the saucer to mark a circle. Cut this out. Draw a line across the centre of the circle and cut it into two equal halves. This is enough to make two extinguishers. The diameter of the cone will depend on the size of the candle you are using. Form your cone to the size you want and trim off any surplus overlapping foil if there is too much. Make a nice fine point, neatly closed. Turn the join in the foil away from you to the rear, so that it will not be seen when on the candle, and pinch the point flat between finger and thumb. This not only keeps the cone together and airtight, but also serves as a little handle with which to pick up the cone. When your ritual is completed, your candles will have been extinguished correctly, and all the candles will have little silver caps on, unless the ritual calls for the candles to burn out naturally.

Dress and Incense

You do not have to wear any special ritual clothes or robes, though you can if you wish. There are, however, certain considerations, based on sound reasoning. The clothes you wear to work literally become 'impregnated' with the stresses and tensions of your everyday work and affairs. Bathe if possible, but always at least wash your hands. No workclothes, please. Some ritualists make up a simple, loose fitting garment, used for ritual work only, either in white or their zodiac color. The purpose of keeping the robe for ritual work only is to avoid cross or bad 'vibrations,' which could make a ritual ineffective or only partially successful. A surgeon does not enter an operating theatre or operate after walking straight in from the street.

Some writers suggest that the best method is the removal of the clothes altogether, saying that they hinder the 'build-up' of the power. I have never found this to be so. Ritually unclean clothes will have a far greater adverse effect.

Incense is an indispensable part of any ritual, as far as I am concerned. Incense creates the right 'atmosphere,' which in turn induces that state of mind conducive to good ritual. For further information, see my *Incense* (Aquarian Press, 1980).

The Moon's Phases

You should try to time certain of your rituals to coincide with the phases of the Moon, using the correct phases according to the type of ritual being operated. For matters in which you want growth, expansion, or development, you use the period when the Moon is 'waxing,' from New Moon to Full, for as the Moon 'grows' so will the matter in which you have an interest. The nearer to the date of the New Moon the better, for as she approaches Full her powers (in this particular phase) are weakening in readiness for her new phase.

For matters in which you wish decrease, diminishing, lessening, or removal, you use a 'waning' Moon, from just after the Full Moon to the Last Quarter. For as she wanes, diminishes, or 'dies' so will that which you seek diminish and 'die' also. You do not use the three days before the actual date of the New Moon. This was termed by the ancients 'the Dark of the Moon.' During this period, things did not go right and could even go in reverse, so avoid this particular period. As far as I am concerned, the other period to avoid is the actual time of the Full Moon itself, unless you are operating a ritual for confusion, disorder, or chaos. This is a time of perplexity when things can appear to be other than they are (it is well known that love and lovers like a Full Moon). Some writers suggest the period of the Full Moon as a time for the development of clairvoyant abilities, but in my opinion this period encourages ability mostly in the lower astral forms of clairvoyance. It is well known that certain mental aberrations can be triggered by the Full Moon, so it is a lower astral working of uncertain worth and its use is not recommended.

The Negative Art of Black Magic Candles

As ritual candles are shown to have their dark, negative side, can the candles be used in Black Magic? The answer to this and all similar questions is, Yes, of course they can. People are quite surprised, and occasionally disbelieving, when they come to the realization that the training of the Black and White Magician is, primarily, the same up to a certain point. Many hold the opinion, which is not untenable, that there is no such thing as Black and White magic – only magic. It is simply a question of whether the veil is legitimately rent from 'top to bottom,' or, by dubious methods, torn from 'bottom to top.' Good and evil pass through the same veil, though for different intent. The difference between the two lies in the use to which the magical training and knowledge are employed.

Black candles are used as the prime source for 'illumination' in the Black Mass, or in any ritual designed to hurt, exact revenge or punishment, or bring chaos and disorder into someone's life. One of the first things you do is to replace your white Altar Candles with black ones to denote the source you are working with, and under.

I think it should be stressed the beautiful form that 'evil' may on occasion take. Without such beauty, evil would win few friends. We have been well advised that the true distinction between the 'beauty' of evil and that of 'good' lay (metaphorically) in the 'temperature of its radiation' – i.e., 'the beauty of evil is a *cold* beauty, and therein *lies the secret.*' Even a fallen angel must, to evolving Man, appear as 'perfection' (for, relative to us, such a one *would* indeed be 'perfect'). Even in our blind, stumbling way, our concern must surely be with ABSOLUTE, and not RELATIVE truth (or 'beauty') – thus it is that we must be ever mindful about to whom, or what, we grant our *allegiance.* Even in English Common Law, if one enters into a *contract* with a person under a delusion about that person's identity, it is not always possible to resile without incurring a PENALTY. This analogy is *not* without point, I feel. Graham Greene made the same (important) point in *The Power and the Glory* – 'But I'm a bad priest, you see I know – from experience – how much beauty Satan carried down with him when he fell. Nobody ever said the fallen angels were the ugly ones . . . .'

What advice do we give to would-be followers of the Lefthand Path? That's simple – don't take it! However, no one can stand over you all the time, to see that you do not yield to these temptations, and why should they, even if they wished? If you *are* hell-bent on the pursuit of this unwholesome and contaminating subject, it *will* be so and any impediment seems to make it more attractive. With increasing interest in all aspects of occultism, people (the young are especially vulnerable) can expose themselves to considerable risk because they are working with forces the untutored find are beyond their control. The learner can be confronted (unexpectedly) with forces, unwittingly or recklessly invoked, he is ill-equipped to handle. The unfailing safeguard is utmost caution and adequate training secured, if possible, under qualified guidance. This has *not* been inserted to alarm or to create an effect in print, merely to counsel that you should go forward by all means, but with great vigilance.

3

THE IMPORTANCE OF COLOR

One of the most important factors in ritual candle work is color. Color belongs to the practice and doctrine of correspondences. Among the first things the beginner in the occult has to understand is the great web of correspondences, how things are linked or connected. It can be likened to an occult ABC. From his earliest beginnings, Man has attempted to understand the manifested universe into which he has been thrust. We use symbolism as an aid to understanding and to try to come to terms with spiritual truths (the Tree of Life is an attempt in this direction) which the untutored mind, unassisted, could not comprehend. Thus symbolism embodies fundamental and primary truths which, if contemplated correctly, enable us to conceive and understand the ideas and potencies behind the symbol and, it is hoped, to make a link with that source, potency, or spirit which will aid us in our understanding of matters that are beyond the ken of our physical senses.

We have on record correspondences of planets, signs of the zodiac, angelic signatures, spirits and intelligences, colors, and so on. From this long, impressive list we shall concern ourselves primarily with color (and with some other matters indirectly) and its use in work with the ritual candles.

The use of color is particularly important in candle work for many reasons. Color is vibration (as with sound) on certain wave lengths, and because of this the eye is able to register and recognise quite subtle changes, thus identifying subtle hues within the basic color. Colors place you 'in tune' with sources or powers of sympathetic vibrations, which is why it is highly desirable to use the correct color and not the wrong one.

The symbolism of color and our response to it, as with so many other things, is dependent upon where we are born and on the nature of our cultural responses. We in the Western hemisphere associate black with death (a color of the planet Saturn who has death under his rulership, among other things). We use this color to denote our loss, sadness, and mourning (all Saturnine aspects). Many Eastern countries and nations, especially the Chinese, use the exact opposite, white, for the same purpose. Blue is associated, in most Christian countries, with heaven and spirituality. The Yezsidi (of Kurdistan, Armenia, and the Caucasus) do not hold this color in the same esteem. In fact they abhor blue, and the worst curse they can heap upon the head of those who offend them is 'may they die and be buried in blue garments!'

These two examples alone would suggest that only a fool would attempt to give any arbitration on this subject, yet it is not as difficult as it may appear at first glance. We have an established tradition of correspondences in the West, a tradition that has endeavoured to build up a physical science of color including that seen by the physical eye and subjective experience. This tradition, however, is often sadly neglected because the grass, as always, looks greener in other fields (often Eastern ones). Let there be no doubt whatsoever that the tradition *is* here, though you will have to work harder to find it, for its roots are buried deep in the good, rich soil of these islands. It is not dead, only 'sleeping' and neglected.

I can only appeal to those who will listen not to encourage that neglect any further. So many people are indifferent to the treasures that lie in their own backyard, thinking instead that they will find them in someone else's. But all they succeed in doing is to cultivate another's vines through the neglect of their own: it is a case of 'the idiot who praises with enthusiastic tone every century but this, and every country but his own.' Yet this curious meiosis seems to be a characteristic British trait. People can choose to neglect their 'Racial Genius' or 'Angel,' into whose charge, for one lifetime at least (possibly more), they are given; but if this Being is systematically neglected by the people and by the nation over which it has Guardianship, then it may well relinquish the Guardianship and finally desert its charges. This can, and will, have disastrous results, and the effect on the people of that nation will, in the final outcome, prove to be an irreparable loss.

Let us take a look at the fundamental colors we shall be using in candle work. One of the first things we must take into consideration, as we have seen, is the seeming contradiction in the meanings attributed to colors. A color which is represented as benevolent at some times is at others represented as being malevolent. Both the problem and the answer lies in, and is explained by, one word – duality, those twin aspects which appear to be inseparable on all the lower planes of existence, affording Mankind the cause of much that ails it – the necessity of making a choice.

For example, pure unmanifested force, represented astrologically by the planet Mars, has no particular axe to grind at its source. It can, however, represent in its positive aspect the knife in the hands of the surgeon, used with skill to ease pain and save life (knives, surgery, and surgeons are all under the rulership of Mars); in its negative aspect, it can represent the knife in the hands of an assassin, perhaps used with equal skill, to inflict pain and deny life (Mars rules blood, blood-letting, bloodshed, and assassins). Hence Mars in its 'positive' aspect represents initiative with constructive action directed to personal or common good, and the surmounting of obstacles to attain success; in its 'negative' aspect, it represents a destructive and wanton contempt for anyone and everything that stands in the way of personal ambition and gain that must be removed without regard or regret.

The color correspondence of the planet Mars is red, and thus it must follow that this color can be used to designate both its positive and negative aspects, a point that sometimes confuses the beginner, though the examples given should clear up this confusion to some extent. (This example can also be extended to the other planetary colors.) This is one of the reasons why (apart from the Sun and Moon) the planets of old astrology were each given two houses and signs, which permitted two modes or channels of operation and expression: positive/negative, light/dark, day/night houses or thrones, and so on.

Many practitioners use brighter and darker hues of the same color to represent these twin aspects. In our example, using Mars, this would be bright red for positive and dark red for negative. This method can add a little confusion to the issue, as dark red is one of the colors that can be used to represent the sign of Scorpio, and dark green the planet Saturn. In my own system I use a bright red candle for the positive aspect, but to represent the negative aspect I drip some black wax on the same candle to show that the positive aspect has been degraded into a negative one. With this method you need only keep the basic colors and not two of each, as you will already have black candles in stock. With this method and a black candle you can make all the positive colors into negative candles in like manner.

Now let us look at the colors we shall use, taken from a wide range of sources.

Black

It is almost impossible to write of black without mentioning white, and vice versa. It is suggested, therefore, that they virtually be read as one. It has been like this since the beginning of time, one color standing diametrically opposed to the other. In Wolfram von Eschenbach's sublime mediaeval poem Parzival, we are told in the opening lines that the spirit of a dauntless man is both black and white 'like a magpie's plumage,' and that these colors have 'a share in him,' representing as they do the colors of heaven and hell. Steadfast thoughts draw near to the brightness of heaven, while inconstancy is black like hell.

Black, however, like most things 'is not as black as it's painted'! Gestation of all kinds takes place in its dark, brooding kingdom. The ideas for this book were formulated there, and the words I write now are being taken from the mind, out of sight, hidden, intangible to all intents and purposes to outsiders until they are finally written down, or brought out 'into the light' for better or worse. The 'seeds' of most of the elemental kingdoms are planted, and initially grow, out of sight, as with precious gems that grow in the depths of the earth until they are mined. The vegetable and animal seeds that are planted in the dark soil and the darkness of the womb are likewise away from light and sight, until finally in due course of time, they emerge and present themselves to the light for growth and evolution in one way or another. Hence, black stands for the initial stages of growth in most things. Many Earth Mothers are for this reason frequently represented with black faces and hands, which we find later transferred to some early Christian Madonnas. H. P. Blavatsky observed that the Bible shows that Noah in the ark upon the waters released a black bird (a raven – the initial stage) first, which did not return, then a white bird (a dove – the later stages), which, finding nowhere to rest, came back. Seven days later when sent out again, she came back in the evening with an olive leaf in her beak, to show Noah that the time was right and it was safe to leave the ark.

Though having made defence of black, the theme is still one of emergence and struggle into light for growth and development which, although black may start the process, white must and usually does finish, or it will perish. For the purposes of candle work the color black is regarded as 'negative,' since it negates colors, actions, thoughts, purpose, and people.

Every pilgrim to Mecca kisses the Kaaba, the most famous and holy stone of the Islamic faith. It is held that the stone was originally white when it fell from heaven, but the sins of mankind turned it black, which implies negation from white to black in its descent to the physical plane. Persian legend gives the stone as an emblem of the planet Saturn. Saturn is the planet of death, sorrow, grief, and mourning. The Romans borrowed the Egyptian idea and custom of wearing black for death and mourning. Although we use the term 'blackguard' in a derogatory sense for rogues and scoundrels, it was the name originally given to the link-boys or torch-bearers at funerals who were more correctly called 'black guards,' or 'blacks,' often mutes wearing black clothes and cloaks. The planet Saturn, however, has excellent positive attributes – including stability and wisdom, and many other positive gifts of old age: control, caution, justice, practicality, thrift, and responsibility.

Black is naturally linked with night and darkness and by extension with death, which is the 'night' that ends a man's 'day' in mourning and sorrow. Black represents evil, the power called Satan and the Powers of Darkness. The Romans marked their lucky days with white chalk, their unlucky ones they marked with charcoal – thus 'black days.' It also came to mean the days which were not auspicious, as distinguished from the saint's days, which were printed in red.

In Greece and Rome, black animals were connected with the Earth Goddess and the 'powers below,' the ghosts of the dead in the Underworld. It is the color of the earth in which we are buried at death. Standing both for death and earth in Alchemy, black represents death and putrefaction, yet also germination and new life burgeoning in the depths and darkness. Renewed life comes to the surface in the 'white' stage of alchemical work. The opposition and contrast of black and white are fundamental to most countries in one way or another, especially to European cultures and their color symbolism. In churches, the black trappings of Good Friday are replaced on Easter Sunday with white to symbolise Christ's Resurrection. On the chess board, black and white knights do battle as they do in myth and legend, which are the lifeblood of any nation. In art, especially religious, we find the Devil and his legions arrayed in black, or very dark colors, the righteous wearing white in heaven.

The following applies to the color black and its *particular* use in ritual candle work. It also represents the negative aspects of the planet Saturn (whose positive aspects follow):

Negative Thoughts:

Depression; melancholy; despondency; despair; sadness; pessimism; discouragement; and so forth.

Negative People:

Those who obstruct and oppose, limit, impede, and hinder. Who are spiteful, hateful, bear rancour, animosity, and malice.

Negative Actions:

Those of detriment, mischief, injury, and damage. Of abuse, sabotage, and ruin. Of slander and libel, disparagement, maligning, derogatory, and defamatory work.

Positive Aspects of Saturn:

Old people, wise in years and council. Stability, control, caution, justice *without* mercy (often Karmic, justice *with* mercy is Jupiter). Patience, practicality, thrift, responsibility and the ability to act as such, and so on.

To represent an 'older' person, you could put the symbol of the planet Saturn on the side of their Zodiac Candle (if you wish). Just remember to keep black, in this work *only*, to represent the negative aspects above – either black on a color or a black candle.

White

White denotes cleanliness, hence purity and innocence. To represent something in white is to show a state of grace and purity, a 'virgin' state (the Vestal Virgins wore white to tend the Sacred Flame). It was a short step from this that the Gods would find white an acceptable color. The Roman priests of Jupiter wore white robes and sacrificed white cattle to him. At the death of a Caesar, the national mourning was white. The sacred horses of the Greek, Roman, Germanic, and Celtic peoples were white. The traditional 'knight in shining armour' always rode on a white horse, the evil knight on a black, with black armour. The god of the ancient Egyptians, Osiris, wore a white crown and his priests were robed in white. In religious art, Christ is usually shown in a white robe after the Resurrection, as are the angels and righteous dead in heaven. In the Church, white is used for festivals of Christ, Maundy Thursday, and for the Saints, though not for the Martyrs. Whit Sunday, or White Sunday, is the seventh Sunday after Easter and commemorates the descent of the Holy Ghost at Pentecost. Its name is supposed to derive from the fact that the aspirants wore white garments. The white tincture of Alchemy is the name given to a preparation that should convert any base metal into silver.

White also has negative qualities attributed to it, as our everyday speech shows, including weakness, infirmity, and cowardice. It draws some of its negative symbolism from the fact that paleness has always been associated with bloodlessness and lack of vigour. So we use the term 'as white as a sheet' of someone who has had a fright which has drawn the blood from the face and lips, while 'lily-livered' or 'white-livered' refers to the popular belief that the liver of a coward is devoid of blood, 'who inwardly searched, have livers white as milk.' All these imply an absence of blood, which gives a white appearance – the white/Moon (female) aspect instead of the red/Mars (male) aspect. To show a 'white feather' was regarded as a sign of cowardice, the term being taken from the old sport of cock-fighting. If the gamecock's tail showed a white feather it was a sign of base breeding. A completely white flag is universally accepted as a sign of surrender to the enemy, a banner of defeat. A 'whited sepulchre' is a person who hides his hypocrisy under a cloak of virtue. Jewish sepulchres were painted white to make them conspicuous, to avoid ritual defilement by someone's approaching too close. Jesus uses the term (Matt. 23:27): 'Ye are like unto whited sepulchres, which indeed appear beautiful outward, but are within full of dead men's bones, and of all uncleanness.'

Examples of the opposition of black and white abound, especially in the occult. The obvious is the right-hand path, which is constructive and white, the left-hand path being destructive and black. The practitioner of the Right is a White Magician, of the Left a Black Magician, an agent of the Devil.

Positive Aspects:

Cleanliness; purity, innocence; good; light; peace; modesty, spirituality, sincerity, truth; spotlessness; sinlessness; innocence; simplicity; and hope.

Negative Aspects:

Weakness; delicacy; infirmity, cowardice; bloodlessness; lack of vigour; lack of life; timidity, enervation; impotence; impurity, spoilt; corruption; and debility.

Red

Red is the color of the planet Mars and pre-eminently the color of blood, which is under his rulership. Mars or Ares is the God of War in which so much blood is spilled. As a result, red stands for physical life and energy. In many prehistoric burials the body was often sprinkled or painted with red ochre to give the corpse life in the afterworld. Many early Indian burials (New World) left the face and genitals unpainted, so the deceased could make free choice which sex they would return as. It often puzzles some students why many female gods have red faces instead of the more usual feminine colors, in particular white. The color was often used as it denoted and represented birth, generation, and creation. The earth was 'created' in fire as a molten mass.

The ideas that people associate with this color are of primitive, uncontrolled passions and emotions, mutiny, rebellion, anarchy, force, ruin, and the breaking up of laws. The red flag of Communism and Socialism, the 'People's Flag, is deepest red,' stained, as it is, with the blood of their martyrs, whose lifeblood 'dyes its every fold.' In the French Revolution, those who wore red caps were known as the 'red revolutionaries,' for they had no hesitation in dying their hands to the elbows in blood. In most countries, red lights and flags denote danger and a warning not to proceed (as with traffic lights), to take warning and desist. Sexuality and lust gave us the 'red light' of the brothel and the 'red light districts' of our cities. In magic, red can be used in its negative aspect in operations of hatred, cruelty, and revenge. Naturally, red can be used in a positive aspect, for

Mars can be defensive as well as offensive. The glowing red fire gave protection against beasts of prey and enemies, and may have strengthened the use of red objects for defence against attack on both the physical and psychic level. A red thread is the mark of a witch.

Red symbolises love, shown in the red vestments of the cardinals of the Christian church as a symbol of Divine Love, whilst the red rose has always been a token of love on the physical plane. In church decoration it is the color used for the Martyrs who suffered martyrdom and bloodshed for their faith. Red is one of the five colors of Chinese symbolism, relating to fire and the south. A Chinese official of highest rank, a Mandarin, wore a red button (of red coral) in his cap as a badge of honour. Chinese and Japanese children always used to wear a touch of red, for it symbolised long life.

In alchemical speech, a 'red man' is the personification of the 'prima materia' of the Philosopher's Stone, used in conjunction with the 'white woman' to express affinity and interaction of chemicals (one of the names given to the Philosopher's Stone was the *red tincture* because with its help it was hoped to transmute base metals into gold). Red and white dragons play an important part in alchemical symbolism. The association of red with the extremes of love and lust is almost universal. Sin in the Bible runs 'scarlet' and lust is the 'scarlet woman' of Revelations. In seventeenth century England an adultress was compelled to wear a scarlet 'A' as a badge of shame.

Red, being an active, exciting color, should not be used (as most hospitals attest) in sick rooms. An exception to this was the use of a 'red room' to try and pull neurotics out of their gloom and despondency. It is generally held that this particular color should not be used around nervous and excitable children. It is a psychological fact that this color has the ability to both attract and repel. Many people have an instinctive dislike of people with red or ginger hair, and in Western civilizations this may be accounted for by the fact that traditionally Judas had red hair. The fact that the fat of a redhaired person was once much in demand as an ingredient for poison may not have helped much. One fact is indisputable – red cannot be ignored!

Positive Aspects:

Heat and warmth; health; strength; sexuality; courage; vigour; love (physical and Divine); exuberance; creations; dynamism; stimulation; enthusiasm; birth; generation; and triumph.

Negative Aspects:

Hatred; lust; anger; passion (uncontrolled and primitive); attack; force; anarchy; rebellion; danger; peril; mutiny; war; blood and its shedding; violence; cruelty, and revenge.

Blue

This is the color of unclouded skies, clear and radiant and as such linked with the heavens and the supreme sky gods. The ancients refer to the blue of the sky as that 'which endures for ever.' As it has long been connected with the sky gods, it is often given as a color for the planet Jupiter (royal blue). The Virgin Mary's robe is frequently blue to emphasise, among other things, her role as 'Queen of Heaven.' Blue is often equated with 'levels,' space, height, and depth – the blue sky above and the blue sea below.

The link with the sky gods has perhaps strengthened the connection of blue with the aristocracy and royalty. A person of high and noble descent claimed 'blue blood.' To be 'true blue' is to be honest, conservative, loyal, and trustworthy. Politically, blue is usually the color of Conservatism, as opposed to the red of Communism and Socialism. The colors of the American Flag (the 'Stars and Stripes') were early and officially defined: white for purity and innocence; red for hardiness and vigour; blue for vigilance, perseverance, and justice.

The Blue Ribbon is the highest honour to be given by the British Crown, as is the Garter the highest honour of the Order of Knighthood. The Blue Riband is the highest honour given in many sports. Many people seek the elusive 'bluebird of happiness.' A 'blue-eyed' boy is a favourite, the one who receives preferential treatment, while the 'blue-eyed Maid' was, according to Homer, the Goddess of Wisdom, Minerva. 'Once in a blue moon' is applied to things that happen very rarely; Indians (New World) thought this only took place about every twenty-one years, when the Sun and Moon were in their most harmonious aspect to each other.

When used in religious painting and art, an angelic robe of this color denoted fidelity and faith. As a mortuary color it signifies eternity when applied to the Deity, and immortality when applied to Man. Pale blue (Christian philosophy) denotes love of good works, prudence, and a serene conscience. Blue is a cold color and so associated with cold, and many drugs that allay inflammation (heat/ red) are given this coloring (cooling/blue). Sensitive people frequently feel tired and depressed when remaining in a room that is predominantly blue, hence the color is avoided by institutions caring for the mentally sick. The color's connection with the sea and water is extended to tears, weeping, and emotional sadness. People have a 'fit of the blues,' and sad and mournful is the music bearing the same name.

Positive Aspects:

Fidelity; inspiration; truth; tranquillity; spiritual understanding; serenity; hope; devotion; calmness; sincerity; intuition; love of Divine Works; and piety.

Negative Aspects:

Coldness; depression; aloofness; melancholy; tears and weeping; emotion; sadness; frigidity; apathy; lack of sympathy; gloom; sorrow; a cooling off (blue) in anything where there was once warmth (red).

Yellow/ Orange

Yellow is a color of many meanings, like the god it represents, the planet Mercury, who has many names – the Archangel Raphael, Hermes Trismegistus, Thoth and Tehuti of the Egyptians, to name but a few. His metal is quicksilver or the 'drywater' of the alchemists, the 'aqua manus non madefaciens' (the water that does not make the hands wet). It is hard to pin down the spirit Mercurius, hence his suitability as the 'Messenger of the Gods.' He has so many facets of an apparently contradictory nature given to him that 'duality' seems almost inappropriate. I am of the opinion that we have lost his measure somewhere in the past, or did we ever have it? We find his color used to represent the color of the Sun and the metal gold, which is the highest metal on the Earth plane, a symbol of perfection, wealth, power, and glory. Pure gold holds form poorly, quicksilver not at all. It takes its shape from whatever it is poured into and promptly changes when poured into another vessel, a true 'shape-changer.' Hence Mercury is 'the trickster' in his negative aspect. Heroes and heroines of the past all had yellow or golden hair. It is the color of luminosity and light and is frequently used for the Sun. You will have noticed, however, that the color primarily used for the Sun is orange; this is because it combines yellow with the 'elemental' color of fire, which is red, for the Sun is a fire planet. The Sun and Mercury are inseparable both astrologically and astronomically, and to some practitioners, especially Qabalists, they are virtually interchangeable. When yellow is combined with red to give orange, the result is invigorating, energizing, emotional, life-giving. Yellow, to many of the ancients, was the animating principle of life. To use yellow for the Sun and to represent gold, etc., is quite acceptable and at one time in England the vernacular term for a golden sovereign was 'a yellow boy' (an appropriate term, for the planet Mercury rules youth in particular).

For this reason we have combined the two colors in our heading because at times the dividing line is hard to find. Both are warm colors and yellow has a bright, cheerful effect, especially on the mental states (the planet Mercury has rulership over the mentality). Some sickrooms are often painted with yellow to achieve the above benefits.

Yellow is a royal color in China and is associated with nobility. It has the meanings of gaiety, joy, faith, glory; it also symbolises cowardice, jealousy (often combined with green), mistrust, and illness. A coward has a 'yellow streak' running down his back. The leaves turn yellow in the autumn, heralding winter, so the color is often associated with dying, death, and decay.

Its link with the planet Mercury as the planet of the intellect, power of the mind, writing, language, alphabets, enhances yellow as the color of mentality. In early Christian times, vestments of saffron were worn in churches on Good Friday, which served as a reminder of the vindictiveness of the Jews in crucifying the Christ. In France, the doors of traitors were daubed with yellow, and in some countries there is a long history of the Jews being made to wear a yellow mark or yellow clothes to distinguish them. In Christian art, Judas is often arrayed in yellow to represent his hate, jealousy, and vindictiveness. In many mediaeval paintings he is frequently given reddish-yellow hair and beard for the same reasons (yellow/jealousy and red/hatred). It is by tradition much the same for Cain.

To be given a 'jaundiced' look is not pleasant, and the yellow of jaundice denoted ill health. By correspondence of 'like curing like' the color was used to try and cure the disease. It was said that if the patient fixed his eye on, gazing into, the large yellow eye of the Stone Curlew, the disease would be transferred to the bird. With all the reference to diseases and their cure, it will come as no surprise that the Archangel Raphael of the planet Mercury is the Great Healing Angel and is invoked in these matters.

Positive Aspects:

Gaiety; life; joy; warmth; strength; glory; cheerfulness; luminosity; light; mentality; the intellect; the power or strength of the mind.

Negative Aspects:

Cowardice; jealousy; distrust; sickness; illness and disease; decay and dying; adultery; perfidy; inconstancy; sickly and sickly looking.

Green

Green is one of the most important colors in Western symbolism, and of the Celtic gods in particular. Throughout the whole of the Western world it symbolises the bounty of Nature, the revival of life after the privation of winter and its cold, deathlike grip on the land. Green is the peace of Nature and thus is generally accepted as a peaceful color. A room painted pale green with some motifs, or parts, painted yellow (color of the mentality) makes for a restful room giving peace of mind and offering protection from adverse thoughts. The 'green room' in a theatre was a waiting room common to all. It was near the stage for the use of performers and was painted green to relieve the eyes from the glare of the stage lighting. Green is the balancing color of the spectrum. It is neither a sad nor cheerful color, but a restful one. It is a bridge between the two halves of the color spectrum, a 'cool' color, coming as it does between the warm colors of red, orange, and yellow, sometimes called the 'approaching or advancing' colors; and the cold colors of blue, indigo, and violet, sometimes called the 'retreating or retiring' colors. It stands midway between yellow and blue, which combine to make it. In Europe we have the Mayday 'Green George,' known to us as 'Jack o' the Green' or 'The Green Man,' and as many inn signs in England attest, there is a strong connection with our own St. George of England. On May Day, a man would dress up in a wicker framework covered with green boughs of holly and ivy, with flowers and ribbons on the top. In many countries he was immersed in water or ducked in the village well to ensure the rain to revive the vegetation and produce lush crops. Holly, ivy, and the evergreens were used because these kept their green foliage throughout the winter, a sign of life, while all other plants appeared to 'die.' They therefore become a symbol of hope, eternal life, and renewal, for they held the 'life' of the vegetation until the Sun returned once more to awaken Nature to be born as new. Our words 'grass,' 'green,' and 'grow' all come from the same root in Anglo-Saxon.

Green, as folklore shows, is the prime color worn by

the 'gentry', the fairy folk, and by many of the people of the Sidhe. Their gods, kings, and queens wore green in contra-distinction to the scarlet cloaks of earthly kings. Green is one of the colors of the planet Venus in her female, moist, dark earthly aspect in the Sign of Taurus, represented by the pastoral bull. I have long thought, however, that this may possibly have been either a mistake or a misinterpre-tation, and that it should have been a pastoral *cow*, sym-bolizing the feminine aspect of the planet in her 'Mother Nature' form (Libra – the Scales – the male aspect), like the Egyptian goddess Hathor – the Egyptian Venus.

In church decoration, green is used to denote God's bounty, gladness, and the Resurrection and is used for weekdays after Trinity. Pale green signifies baptism. Some ancient manuscripts say that the Holy Grail is green, made from an emerald that fell from the brow of Lucifer in his 'fall.' In von Eschenbach's *Parzival,* the Grail is carried in a green achmadi (a piece of green silk material), and green vegetation is connected with the Grail and the Fisher or Grail King. When the correct questions are asked, the King is healed and the land restored to life, showing green once again after the death and famine that has afflicted it.

The color green is the 'benedicta viriditas' (the blessed green) of Alchemy and is deemed to be the color of the Holy Ghost. To be given 'the green light' means you can proceed in safety. Successful gardeners have 'green fin-gers.' For construction and recuperation, green is a won-der, symbolic of hope, life, peace, adaptation, the reflective mind, and the higher mental faculties.

It is the symbol of energy, fertility, new life, growth,

charity. It is refreshing and cool, suggesting peace and relaxation. A 'green old age' is one in which the mental faculties are not impaired. Man's first environment was green – the 'Garden.' When green is darkened with black it denotes envy, jealousy, suspicion, and superstition. 'Green with envy' is an expression used to denote this. Last, and by no means least, there is the Tabula Smaragdina – the Emerald Tablet of the Thrice Great Hermes – which could answer so much.

Positive Aspects:

Calm; pastoral; immortality; eternal youth; budding; stability; productive of joy; gladness; tranquillity; growth; spring; abundance; fertility; balance; and life.

Negative Aspects:

Jealousy; envy; sickness ('green around the gills'); avarice; cowardice; anger; discord; strife; disharmony; suspicion; resentment.

Note:

Many practitioners suggest a green candle for luck in general and money luck in particular, instead of a purple candle for the planet Jupiter. It is a point of view with which I do not completely agree. Most of the above shows the main attributes to be of 'growth and fertility,' thus it should be combined, if you use it, with a candle appropriate in color to the matter in which you wish these things to manifest, for instance, a green candle with a purple candle/Jupiter: for financial growth and gain; a green and pink candle/Venus: for joy, growth, and fertility in love or affairs of the heart; a green and white or silver candle/Moon: for growth of the imagination, natural clairvoyance, or of feminine affairs; a green and black candle for limitation, restriction of growth, to impede and stifle growth and movement. These examples demonstrate how you can both usefully and successfully combine two candles together of the required colors, or alternatively put two colors on a white candle base, or one color on the other.

Pink/Rose

These are the colors of love, being the colors of the planet Venus and her Sign of Libra, which is the natural ruler and sign of the seventh house of the horoscope which rules the social aspects of life, marriage, and all kinds of partnerships. These colors are emblematic of the idealised virtues of romance, gentleness, and affection. This is because red has been mixed with white, the addition of white making the red less destructive and impetuous, less self-centred and less stimulating. This makes the color cheerful and less impassioned. It has been transmuted into a more perfect form by this positive blending. To be 'in the pink' is to be in excellent health, pink skin denoting that the person is not 'off color.' It is the color of modesty. Rose, as a color, is the higher vibration of red and represents beauty, hope, love, and morality.

Grey/Silver-Grey

Grey is often thought of as a neutral color or, lying as it does between black and white, a 'bridging' one, either containing equal parts or with one or the other color predominating. It is used to denote age, maturity, and wisdom in its positive aspect; dotage, senility, or second childhood in its negative age: it can bring either gift. Maturity or old age brings grey or silver hair. Grey often represents mourning. Its neutrality is thought to be due to the addition of the white to black, and thus was representative of the overcoming or mitigation of evil. For much the same reason it frequently depicts cancellation or stalemate, one color cancelling the other out with neither gaining control. White is lively; black is gloomy; grey is intermediate. It is the color of indifference and inertia – the color of the ashes which are left when the fire has burnt out. To 'feel grey' is to be depressed, in a dull state of mind, lacking vitality and color (as an overcast day), to be in the Slough of Despond. At times we all have 'grey areas' in our lives when we are not quite sure whether a thing is black or white, evil or good. Sometimes when we want to do something we feel we should not, we place the matter in the grey area of our conscience.

Brown

The association of this color with the earth links it with solidarity, practicality, and solidity – planting in good rich soil for fruitfulness and growth. Brown moods are those of sadness and melancholy, an absence of mind and thought, a sombre reverie, a musing of only apparent thought. To be 'browned off' is to be fed up or bored. This color has strong associations with autumn and the 'last leaf', brown and wilting before it falls. This is one of the colors of the sign of Virgo, the natural sign of the zodiac in which summer transmutes into autumn (hence the reason why the sign is a 'mutable' one). Everything begins to slow down in preparation for the winter sleep.

A group of the hearth and home spirits of the 'secret commonwealth' are the brownies, the brown or tawny spirits whose favourite abodes are the hearths and farmhouses of the country, and who busy themselves during the night on little jobs for the family for small payment. The best reward is a bowl of cream and a hot cake that has been smeared with honey, 'a piece of wad to please the brownie'! They hate any show of generosity and will leave any house where the owner is rude enough to leave out a suit of clothes for the little, naked helpers.

Purple

This color was frequently a synonym for the Emperor of the Romans. A possible explanation is that because in ancient times purple was an extremely expensive color, only royalty, magistrates, military commanders, and the very rich could afford to wear it. It became a symbol of luxury and power. The color was obtained from the shellfish, *buccinum murex*, the deep color called *'purpureum'* being the name of one of the molluscs. Under the dominion of the planet Jupiter, it has always signified loyalty, majesty, riches, the 'top people' of both wealth and authority (as with the Sun). The planet Jupiter is likewise the ruler of religions, philosophy, all matters that stimulate and occupy the higher mind as opposed to the lower. A spiritual, psychic color endowed with wisdom, reverence, idealism, and dignity, of both office and self, it also denotes meditation and aspiration.

Purple as such is a fairly neutral color, being neither 'warm' nor 'cold,' for it combines red (warm) and blue (cold). Red is the symbol of the Egyptian afterlife and blue the color of eternity. Jupiter links the color with riches and financial success, and in addition it represents stocks, shares, and the stock exchange. Although the vestments of a cardinal are actually red, a priest when elevated to this high rank is said 'to be raised to the purple.'

Purple, therefore, means success, elevation, social prominence and prestige, and the attainment of the heart's desire. Its negative use would be in a tyrannical and despotic abuse of power or authority, a sycophantic seeking of advancement and power, and so forth.

Violet

The plant of this name is said to have sprung from the blood of Ajax. Napoleon Bonaparte was nicknamed 'Corporal Violet,' which became a password and toast for his sympathisers, and by its use they recognised each other. Because of this the Bourbons banned the color as a sign of treachery.

As with all this group of colors, violet is another regal color. It is the color of sacrifice and perseverance, piety and sentimentality. It is a subduing hue and can act as a sedative, producing lethargy, melancholia, and sleep, and as a tranquillizing agent. Regarded as a serious color, it often causes brooding and sadness. To the ancients it symbolised the 'Raiment of God' and as such was held sacred. Symbolic of innocence, a love of truth, and the truth of love, it has the ability to reach lofty heights but is frequently veiled in mystery. Leonardo da Vinci, who knew something about color, said that the power of meditation is ten times greater under violet light falling through the stained glass windows of a quiet church. Count St. Germain is reputed to have used this color in healing and to have removed blemishes from gems and precious stones.

Lavender

The plant of this name was used by laundresses to scent linen and even today it is used by people to scent their bathwater. It is another color of spirituality, being purple tinted with white. As such it is a soothing, dainty color, a token of affection. A pure lavender color is held to be positive, a pure violet color negative.

4

CANDLE RITUALS

In this chapter we shall deal with the ritualistic aspect of candle work, giving example rituals. On no account must these be taken as the only way in which things can be done, though they are fairly representative of traditional rituals as given in older works, and are thus to be found in most modern ones. Create, alter, modify, and personalise them to suit your own needs, circumstances, and temperament. This type of ritual has been practised virtually since mankind discovered the element of fire, though this is not the place to theorise on precisely *how* they work, they simply do. Candle rituals are basically simple, and perhaps this has been their quiet strength. They are available to all, for anyone can perform them with the simplest materials.

I believe simplicity to be the strength of candle work and it is quite often one of the prime reasons why some people disdain its use, especially those who feel (or think) they have outgrown such simple ritual forms and term them 'Low Magic.' Many writers are of the opinion that Low Magic does not involve the use of ritual, yet candle work contains both of these seemingly contradictory aspects. I am certain that the term 'Low Magic' was never intended to have the derogatory sound or meaning people customarily give to it. Never scorn the ladder by which you climb, especially if it is a good strong ladder, for you will find it supports everything that follows. This contempt or disdain for things 'beneath them' is why perhaps so many of the 'mighty' fall in the later stages.

So away with theories, in favour of the simple expedience of 'getting on with it.' Remember, a single, sincere candle (often in an emergency) frequently achieves more than an empty display of ritual, no matter how elaborate. Keep a notebook, a 'Ritual Diary,' and write down *full details* of everything that you do regarding the ritual. Do not neglect your 'feelings' at the time; in retrospect they can often be quite revealing. Record the reason for the ritual; the angels, powers, or spirits invoked; and the relevant details and times. Record anything unusual that may have occurred. Write all the relevant information on one side of the notebook, leaving the pages on the other side blank for writing down any observations. Be absolutely honest in all this; if you are not, never forget that the only person you are fooling will be yourself. Check every aspect or 'result' critically for possible physical explanation, 'trick-of-the-light' effect, or any other explanation, by playing, or getting someone else to play, the Devil's Advocate. Always remember that the 'scavengers' of the Lower Astral, attracted by your 'fire,' are ever alert and optimistic of any means of prolonging their existence close to the Earth plane to which they elect to be bound, and will come and watch your efforts. Should you prove to be a person who can be hoodwinked by their wiles, they will, by their limited but at times most effective machinations, hold you in their thrall and by their tinsel and glamour effects draw the necessary means of sustenance from you and your work.

The touchstone to use is to learn to discriminate between what you want and what you *actually need* in important matters. That may seem a simple enough edict, yet it is one area of human deliberation where discretion and discrimination are required to be at their strongest. We do not, conveniently, always see the difference between what we need and what we want. The Higher Principles, however, that have this planet and mankind in their charge, can detect the slightest trace of negative aspiration in your invocations, so do not entertain any doubts in that particular direction. They may give you (at times) what you *want* (it is quite often a double-edged sword), but often the 'bill' is a salutory lesson. (I am not, however, implying that every little infraction of the rules, every little negative thought or action, is immediately or subsequently karmically avenged from on High. To live like this, or to try to swathe ourselves in cottonwool, would make our lives a mere existence, and an existence can be endured but never lived.) In the actual rituals, perhaps one of the most important requisites is that the candles be extinguished in the reverse order to that of lighting (though not always so, since there are exceptions to every rule), so you must remember the order. The world will *not* stop by making a mistake in this, but you can avoid making the mistake in the first place. If it will help, write the order on a sheet of paper. Make a Ritual Notebook, a companion to your Ritual Diary, containing a diagram of your altar, set out for specific rituals with numbers in circles representing the candles, their positions, and the order of their lighting (see diagrams given). Put a key below each diagram to explain it in full.

Sometimes I use a small ritual which I devised for the lighting of my altar candles, which you may care to use or to employ as a pattern for one of your own devising. It uses, and is based upon, the opening lines of the Book of Genesis, for in your own small way you are trying to 'create,' to bring order out of chaos, to bring light into darkness by uttering the FIAT LUX, those wonderful words, 'LET THERE BE LIGHT.'

Set out your altar for the ritual: if this sounds like chess, the analogy is fair. In chess we have certain concepts and basic objectives which are not incompatible with the aims of many simple rituals. In simple candle ritual, we make moves, using candles instead of chess men, and the 'board' is our altar. To extend this useful analogy, we protect those who are in trouble by moving the correct candles (chess men) to safeguard and fortify that person (or ourselves) in times of onslaught, attack, or trouble by ritual moves, protecting and defending, repulsing and resisting by the angels and powers invoked by ritual (powerful or more mobile pieces that will defend or nullify our opponents' design or the prevailing circumstances).

We protect ourselves and others against the attack of known, suspected, or unknown evil by interposing a candle between ourselves or someone else (Zodiac Candles) and the represented evil (usually a black candle, or a positive candle degraded into its negative aspect by black wax, e.g., jealousy and envy: green/black candle).

We use candles of light and protection until we are, symbolically, ringed by them or within a bulwark of protection and safety. Attraction is symbolised by drawing the candles together; separation and divorce by intervention and interruption; protection by interception and obstruction.

First, set out your altar and your candles. Your room should be as dark as you can make it, especially during the day, in order to aid concentration. Light your incense. Sit for a while in the darkness, contemplating it, closing your eyes if you wish. Try to imagine all life being like this, in darkness as it was 'In the Beginning,' chaos ruling, without light. When you feel ready, say (aloud or mentally) the opening words of Genesis: 'In the beginning God created the heaven and the earth' (this is the first physically manifested act of duality or division by Creation and Order). 'And the earth was without form and void; and darkness was on the face of the deep' (pause here for a while). 'And the Spirit of God moved upon the face of the waters' (pause here and feel, if you can, a light breath or stirring around you). 'And God said, 'Let there be Light' (reach out and pick up your matches, placed ready, and strike one). The light's flaring may temporarily blind you, which is the desired effect. Try to visualise your small act as the 'Beginning,' the darkness pierced by light; imagine the power of those words, their meaning and awesome results. When your flame is secure and the match properly burning, light your altar candles, saying, 'And God saw the light, that it was good: and God called the light Day, and the darkness he called Night. And evening and morning were the first day.' Symbolically, this act is the 'first day' of *your* ritual, in which you are attempting an act of creation (perhaps trying to bring order out of chaos?). In this 'first day' of the Bible, we have the second division (after the division of the heaven and earth): that of day/white and night/black, as discussed in the section dealing with color.

From this point in the ritual I use no more matches, preferring tapers or spills to transfer the flame of the Altar Candles to the remaining candles as required. You can take the light of the Altar Candles to light the lesser candles on your altar (Zodiac and Offertory Candles). You *never* light the Altar Candles from these lesser lights. If the construction of the ritual (as it occasionally may) dictates that the Altar Candles are lit later and not first, as is usual, they are always lit by matches struck for that purpose alone and for those candles only, so that they are lit with 'new fire.' Although you may take the light of the Altar Candles to light other candles on the altar, there is one *strict* exception to this rule which you never do. The lighting of black candles is *never* taken from the Altar Candles but from 'another source.' Black candles are lit from matches struck for that purpose and that match is *not* used for lighting any other candles on the altar.

Ritual Devised for a Newborn Child (Figure 2)

Required: Incense; Altar Candles; seven Angelic/Planetary Candles; (one each of orange; white; red; yellow; purple; blue; and dark green); one white candle made negative with black wax, or one black candle; three white candles; one Zodiac Candle (according to the date of birth of the infant).

Duration: The duration of the ritual is seven days, not continuous (only the Novena Ritual is continuous).

N.B.: Abbreviations used throughout this ritual and all subsequent rituals are as follows: A/C – Altar Candles; Z/C – Zodiac Candles; O/C – Offertory Candles.

Start this ritual on the day the baby is born and burn the candles (Angelic/Planetary) in strict color/day of the week order from the day you start until the sequence of seven is completed, taking seven days to do so. If, for this particular ritual, you cannot start on the day the child is born, then start it the *same day* one week later and complete the ritual in seven days from then.

First Day:

Set out your altar; inclining your head with a nod or a bow to the altar, take three steps towards it (if space is at a premium because the room is small, do it mentally), nod or bow once more, acknowledging the 'Presence.' Always

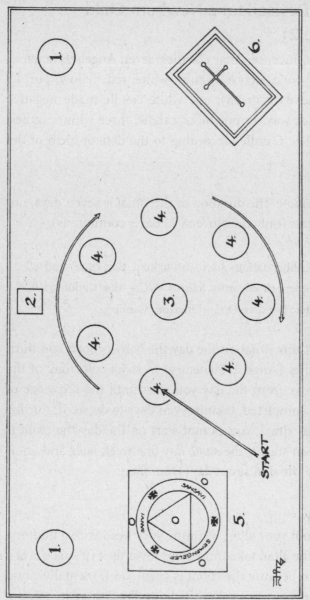

1. Altar Candles 2. Incense 3. Zodiac Candle 4. Angelic Candles 5. Lilith Talisman 6. Bible (optional)

Figure 2

start in this manner no matter what your religious philosophy. Light the A/Cs and devise a small prayer to 'open the ritual' while you light them, to ask a blessing on the work that you are undertaking. This may be of a length and in such words as you feel appropriate. A simple Christian form could take the following lines. At the places marked (+) make a balanced cross over your altar and the candles. 'In the name of God the Father-Mother (+), God the Son (+) and God the Holy Ghost (+), to whom this work is dedicated and from whom a blessing is asked.' You can add to this if you feel that it is too short, yet it declares quite simply your intent and the Source you are working under.

Light the Z/C on behalf of the child, using the child's name if known. Recite or write (on parchment preferably) Psalm 127, placing it under the child's pillow if possible at this point. Now light the Lilith Candle, place it on the talisman (see Figure 3), and say something like: 'Lord God, as in the beginning did Lilith wax hot in anger and spite against the issue of Eve, send, Almighty God, thy three mighty angels, Sanvi, Sansanvi, and Semengalef, to protect this child and stay Lilith's hand against all ill intent and harm.' Light your Lilith Candle with a separate light, not from your A/Cs. Now light the three white candles of the three angels, reciting something similar to the following: 'I call upon thee, the three mighty angels of the Lord our God, to assist me against any attempts of the Dark Moon Lilith to blight or harm the life of this newborn child.' Invoke the angels individually. 'We invoke thee Angel Sanvi' (light one candle from one of the A/Cs); 'We invoke thee Angel Sansanvi' (light the next candle, placing it next

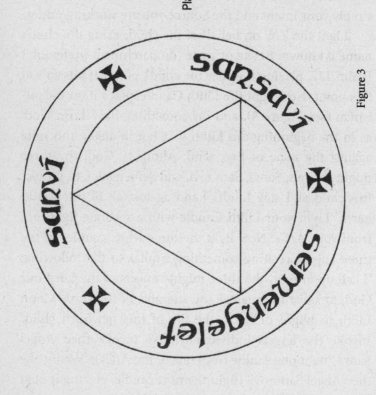

Place black Lilith Candle in the centre of the triangle.

Place the white Angelic Candles outside the circle at the Angels' names (see text).

Figure 3

to the angel's name in a clockwise direction on the talisman – see Figure 3); 'We invoke thee Angel Semengalef (light the last candle and place it on the talisman) to bind Lilith and contain her so that her evil intent is negated and contained within the talisman created in thy names and in the name of the Creator of All.'

Next light the first Angelic/Planetary Candle. We are, for the purpose of this example, taking Sunday as the day of the child's birth. The first angel (one of the child's Guardian Angels, according to the day of birth) will be the Archangel Michael, Angel of the Sun, and so we use an orange candle. The manner and style in which these angels are invoked should be kept reasonably consistent throughout the whole ritual. Something akin to the following may serve as a pattern. 'Lord Michael, Archangel of the Sun, look with grace and favour upon this child [insert name], giving him [or her] the gift of life and your blessing(s) of [insert the particular blessings or gifts you would like to be granted, according to the matters ruled over by the angel].' The various lists throughout the book will help you to decide what you would like these to be. You allow the angel's candle to burn down to the first mark (see the notes below). When this mark is reached, extinguish all the candles in the reverse order to that of lighting. The A/Cs will of course be the last. Allow them to burn for a little while on their own before 'closing the ritual' with another short prayer, which can be the same as the opening one, if you wish. Then extinguish the A/Cs. Stand before your altar for a while; do not walk away. Incline your head or bow to the altar as before, take three steps backwards, and incline your head or bow once more (all of which acknowledges, as before, the 'Presence'). Then retire. As before, if you have limited space that makes these three steps unpractical, make them mentally. Being good ritual practice, it is suggested that you retain it for all your rituals.

Second Day:

All the remaining days take the above form up to the point of lighting the next angel's candle. In our example, the next day would be Monday, ruled by the Archangel of the Moon, Gabriel, and therefore a white candle is used. You would light the candle for the Archangel Michael first and then transfer the flame to the second candle for the Archangel Gabriel, saying in similar fashion to the above: 'Lord Gabriel, Archangel of the Moon, look with grace and favour upon this child [insert name]. Give him/her the gift of life and your blessing(s) of [insert blessings desired].' Once again you insert the blessings, attributes, or gifts, according to the matters ruled by this particular angel, that you would like him to impart. The same procedure is followed for the remainder of the angels for all the following days of the week. Each day you pass the flame from the first Angelic Candle to the second, the next day from the first to the second, and then to the third, and so on. Always bear in mind this concept of 'passing on the light' to create continuity.

Each day of the ritual burns the candles down one mark, until we reach the seventh and last day of the ritual. On this day the candles burn themselves out naturally. The final day of the ritual has all the candles lit on the altar, the seven Angelic/Planetary Candles alight and circling the Z/C of the newborn child. They will, because of the order and manner of burning, have a 'stepped' appearance representative of a ladder or staircase by which the child may 'climb to life,' with, one hopes, the Angelic and Planetary blessings invoked on its behalf.

On the last day of the ritual the first Angelic/Planetary Candle (Sunday's) has only one mark left, the next (Monday's) two, the next (Tuesday's) three, and so on to the last and seventh candle, which has all seven marks left to burn. It would be better to use a slightly smaller candle for Lilith than the rest, so that she is still 'guarded' by the three angels' candles when she goes out. It does not really matter at what point in the ritual this happens. Similarly, the child's Z/C will still be protected from her by the seven lit Angelic Candles.

Notes

These notes, although applying principally to this ritual, are fairly general and will be found to apply to most candle work and the rituals that follow.

One thing that often perplexes the beginner is how long to let a candle burn for each time period when the ritual is continued into the next day (the candles being extinguished after the first day and re-lit on each of the remaining days of the ritual). This is easy enough to resolve by simply putting small marks on the side of the candles (never the A/Cs) in similar fashion to a 'clock candle,' each section representing one period of the ritual according to the number of days the ritual lasts. A four-day ritual simply divides the candle into four equal parts, whereas for a seven-day one you would simply measure and divide your candle into seven equal parts, by putting small horizontal marks on the candle, and so on. An excellent tool for inscribing your candles, as previously mentioned, is an exhausted fine-pointed ballpoint pen, which writes neatly and easily on the candle wax. Turn the marks to one side so they can just be seen. *Never* (apart from the A/Cs, which are permanent as the Deity they represent) start a new ritual with old candles left over from a previous one; always use fresh candles. When you buy your candles (if you do not make them), try to know the price beforehand so as to give the correct money and thus receive no change. This is very old practice. If you *do* have to receive change, walk out and leave it. If you do take it, then put it in the first charity box you see, but do not keep it or use it. Throw it into some water, e.g., a pond, river, or stream.

Angelic Signatures and Planetary Signs

You can mark your Angelic and Planetary Candles with the angel's signature and/or planetary sigils (see Tables) even though you are burning the correct planetary color. Angelic and Planetary Candles can be marked thus to differentiate them from the A/Cs, which can be of the same color. Write the designs on the side of the candle with your ballpoint pen, from wick to base, so that it begins with the light. If you want the design to be prominent, then do as I do, paint it in with a small brush, using the small pots of model paint (black can be used for this). If you ever run out of colored candles (or a particular color), you can mark white candles with the appropriate signs and fill in the symbols with the *correct color* with your paint, this time on the white wax (e.g., Jupiter/Sagittarius/Pisces – purple; Sun/Leo – orange; Venus/Taurus/Libra – light blue or green, and so on).

Lilith

Lilith, according to Talmudic tradition, is the 'Queen of Evil,' the 'Mother of Demons and the Dark Moon,' which is the reason for her being represented by a white candle negated with black wax, or a black candle. She was the first wife of Adam, who quarrelled with and left him 'waxing hot with anger.' She went off to the shores of the Red Sea and there coupled with lascivious demons, eventually giving birth to a brood of demons known as the 'liliot' or 'linilim,' at the prodigious rate of over one hundred a day. Adam's complaint to God about her running off and her refusal to come back caused Eve to be created for Adam in Lilith's place. Three angels were sent after her to bring her back, but once more and in great wrath she refused to return. This rage against Adam and his new (second) wife Eve resulted in her venting her fury upon their children and all subsequent generations. Whereas Lilith is a destructive force that spawned demons (the Talmud says she was created from 'filth and slime'), Eve is constructive and the Mother of all Humanity (she was created from the flesh and blood of Adam himself). It is generally thought

sunday :: ⊙ :: ♌ :: michael :: 𝔐𝔦𝔠𝔥𝔞𝔢𝔩

monday :: ☽ :: ♋ :: gabriel :: 𝔊𝔞𝔟𝔯𝔦𝔢𝔩

tuesday :: ♂ :: ♈♏ :: samael :: 𝔖𝔞𝔪𝔞𝔢𝔩

wednes" :: ☿ :: ♊♍ :: raphael :: 𝔯𝔞𝔭𝔥𝔞𝔢𝔩

thurs" :: ♃ :: ♐♓ :: sachiel :: 𝔖𝔞𝔠𝔥𝔦𝔢𝔩

friday :: ♀ :: ♉♎ :: anael :: 𝔞𝔫𝔞𝔢𝔩

satur" :: ♄ :: ♑♒ :: cassiel :: 𝔠𝔞𝔰𝔰𝔦𝔢𝔩

Figure 4

that it was Lilith who caused Cain's fury against his brother Abel so that he rose up and slew him.

People in many parts of the world today still wear amulets representing the three angels who were sent after Lilith (called Sanvi, Sansanvi, and Semengalef) to preserve them against the hatred of Lilith against their children and against the temptation and seduction by Lilith (or Lilah as she is also called, perhaps giving us De-Lilah, likewise a seductress and temptress). These talismans are worn because, although Lilith refused to return, she gave her promise to these three angels that if she saw their three names written beside a newborn babe, she would withhold her hand and spare it – the purpose of the ritual. A typical talisman is a magical circle with the words 'Adam and Eve barring Lilith,' usually drawn in charcoal on the wall of the room in which the child lies, with the three angelic names written on the door. The alternative, 'Let not Lilith enter here,' is frequently written over the head of the bed of an expectant mother in red (the protective color of the planet Mars). She seems, naturally, but unfairly, more kindly disposed to girls, for they are only at risk from her hostility until they are twenty days old. The boys, however, are not free from her wiles and malevolence until their eighth birthday.

A Talisman for Protection from Lilith

If you wish to make an altar talisman against Lilith, and it need not be restricted to this use, it may be done in the following manner. Take a sheet of strong white paper (size depending upon space available). Draw a large circle on it in black, and inside this circle draw another one slightly smaller. Divide this inner circle into three equal parts of 120° and make small marks at these points. Join these marks together to make a triangle in the centre of the talisman. At the three points where the triangle touches the inner circle, in between the inner and the outer circle, write the three angelic names, Sanvi, Sansanvi, and Semengalef, in a clockwise direction, one at each point of the triangle. Midway between these names, draw a balanced cross. Place this talisman on your altar on the left-hand side. Place the candle for Lilith in the centre of the triangle, with one white candle for each of the three angels outside the outer circle, opposite their names (you can mark the candles if you so wish) at a point of the triangle. Only one thing must be observed *without fail* with this, or any other talisman for that matter: the outer circle *must* be complete with no gaps in it. Make this outer circle extra heavy if necessary to achieve this. If you are trying to contain something there must be no gaps or breaks through which it can escape or elude you.

Rituals of Attraction (See Figure 5)

I shall not be giving individual rituals for all the various matters we consider important in our lives because the basic concept is the same for most rituals of this type, varied only by conditions prevailing at the time of the ritual, personal temperament, and philosophy. Only the candles vary in accordance to what we wish to attract: Zodiac

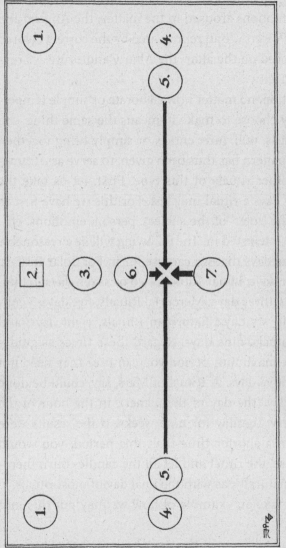

1. Altar Candles 2. Incense 3. Candle of ritualist 4. Candle of petitioner
5. Negative green/black Candles 6. Venus/pink Candle 7. Venus/light green Candle

Figure 5

Candles are for people; Offertory Candles for the affairs concerning those people, their hopes and wishes, the feelings and emotions aroused in the matter; the Angelic and Planetary Powers are all represented by the correct colored candles placed on the altar; the Altar Candles always represent the Deity.

Attraction, no matter how elaborate or simple temperament may choose to make it, means the same thing – to draw towards, pull, lure, entice, or simply bring together. One basic pattern has thus been given, to serve as a framework for other rituals of this type. First, let us take the number of days a ritual may last. For this we have first to ascertain the 'ruler' of the subject, person, emotions, etc., that we are interested in. The following will be a reasonable guide to the days that we can use for it. For Solar Rituals, one or four days; Lunar Rituals, two or seven days; Jupiterian Rituals, three days; Mercurial Rituals, five days; Venusian Rituals, six days; Saturnian Rituals, eight days; and Martian Rituals, nine days. Regard these times as guidelines to the maximum period you can use. They need not be consecutive days. A Ritual of Mars, say, could be done on a Tuesday (the day of the planet), in the hour of the planet, every Tuesday for nine weeks. If the results were achieved in a shorter time than this period, you would simply 'close' the ritual and let all the candles burn themselves out naturally, as with the final day of most rituals.

Let us take an example of how we may put this into practice.

We shall take one of the three basic wishes of humanity to which most requests boil down; love, health, and wealth. In this particular instance we shall take love. Let us assume it is desired to try and bring together or bring love to people who have a barrier of suspicion and mistrust between them. I stress that this must be done with the consent of both people or you will be guilty of 'mental trespassing,' to quote a respected writer. There also has to be the desire for the attraction or the possibility of attraction between them.

Now look at your diagram. Use an incense of Venus, or at least, a heavy, sweet-smelling, rather sensuous one. In the manner given in the previous notes, light the A/Cs. Light the Candles of Distrust and Suspicion; next light the Z/C, representing yourself, the ritualist. At the end of the altar the two Z/Cs, which represent the petitioners, are placed behind the negative Candles of Distrust and Suspicion. They should be as far apart as your altar permits. The common ground in the centre of the altar is the place in which you are trying to bring them to meet. As a Venus Ritual can last six days, you will have to mentally divide up or mark the altar along an imaginary line across the centre, left to right, a total of six equal moves, so that on the final day and move of the ritual, the candles are together and touching if possible. Likewise, the candles will be divided into six marked sections, so that on the final day, as they are moved for the last time, together and touching, the ritual ends and the last section of each candle burns out. Suspicion and mistrust are represented by a negative green/black candle, placed between and in front of them so that it blocks the two Z/Cs. If the negation comes from only one person, and if this is known, put the green/black candle in front of that person; but if it is mutual, then a green/black candle goes in front of both. We light the green/black candles first, so that they burn out first. Because they are burning lower, the Z/Cs will be able to 'look over' the top of mistrust and suspicion and be able to 'see' each other, as two people seeing each other in the distance, aware of each other's existence. On the last day of the ritual, the Candles of Mistrust and Suspicion should have burnt out first. The two Z/Cs can meet with nothing intervening, with the pink and green candles of Venus to represent the growth (green positive) of love (pink positive) on either side of them, and replacing the negative candles which are no longer there.

In a ritual for money, place a Z/C in the centre of the altar, representing the petitioner who wishes to draw money to him. The money is represented by Jupiter (purple) candles and/or Solar (orange) candles, or a combination of these colors on a white candle base, during a one-, three- or four-day ritual. If there is an obstruction to the flow of money by something or someone, show the obstruction by negative O/Cs, denoting the type of obstruction. Take the negative planetary aspects (ascertain this from the negative color lists and elsewhere), using black wax on the positive color to symbolise this, as usual. If it is a particular person, then use a negative Z/C to denote that person. You would remove the 'obstacles' in similar manner to the above green/black candles, so that the O/Cs (Jupiter/Sun – 'the money') can be drawn to the Z/C (the person). It is not necessary to have a Z/C representing yourself this time, unless you are performing the ritual for yourself, when it would be your Z/C in the centre of the altar, to which the money candles are being drawn. If it were for love, then the O/Cs would be pink or blue (Venus); for success, orange (Sun); for initiative and courage, red (Mars); and so on. But let us return to our example.

Required:

Incense; A/Cs; one Z/C (for the ritualist, according to the birth sign); two Z/Cs (for the people concerned, according to their birth signs); two negative green/black candles (of 'mistrust and suspicion'); one pink candle ('positive love'); one light-green candle ('positive growth').

Duration of the Ritual:

Six consecutive days (or each Friday for six weeks), all performed in the hours of Venus/Angel Anael.

First Day:

Start on Friday in any convenient hour of Venus. Light your incense, then your A/Cs, using your opening prayer to open the ritual as before. Light your Candles of Suspicion and Mistrust and let these burn for a while. Light the Z/C of the ritualist (the ritualist should now contemplate the scene of negative emotion, suspicion, and mistrust, and its results). Light the two Z/Cs on behalf of the petitioners, name them and the circumstances for doing so (which you know best: form it in your own words), and the desire to remove the negative atmosphere. Then, when near the first mark, move the two Z/Cs and their negative candles inwards, towards each other (one day's division).

Burn to the first mark and then extinguish in the reverse order to that of lighting them.

The remaining days of the Ritual are performed in exactly the same way – using the hour of Venus on the next day, which is Saturday, then the hour of Venus on Sunday, and so on until the six days are completed on Thursday. Taking the previous examples mentioned: for money, you would start on Thursday in the hour of Jupiter (but do not forget you could also use the hour of the Sun); for love, as above; for success, you start on Sunday in the hours of the Sun (Thursday and Jupiter can be used alternatively); for initiative and courage you start on Tuesday, in the hours of Mars; and so on. The system is the same, which is why it has been stressed how important it is to know who rules what and why.

Back to our example ritual. By the time you have reached the sixth and last day of the ritual, the negative Candles of Suspicion and Mistrust should have been removed because they are burnt out, and the Z/Cs brought together – the purpose of the ritual. On about the fourth or fifth day, say, you place the green and pink candles, as in the diagram, and move these forward so that they meet in the centre of the altar. These replace the negative candles and represent the growth of love (they will flank on either side the Z/Cs). All the candles are to burn out naturally as usual; then extinguish the A/Cs. When you do this, close the ritual with your prayer and leave your altar in the ritual manner.

Rituals of Banishment (See Figure 6)

As with the Ritual of Attraction, we give a basic ritual from which the reader will have little or no trouble in constructing a similar one for any particular purpose. 'Banishment' means the act of eliminating, dismissing, expulsion, or exclusion. Let us take a common case, and one in which we are frequently asked to assist: the banishment of evil, or evil influences.

The evil, if known, can be represented by the appropriate candles, so let us take some examples of this. If the evil is a jealous or envious person who is *definitely known*, he or she can be represented by the appropriate Z/C, one on which you have put some black wax to show the evil intent. Jealousy can be symbolised by a dark green/black candle and/or envy by a yellow/black candle, flanking the negated Z/C; hatred and animosity by a red (dark red if you wish) candle, again with black wax. For a despotic, tyrannical person who is, by his authority, making life unbearable by its misuse, use orange/black or purple/black, and so on.

You can stand these candles next to the appropriate Z/C (if known), or they can be used by themselves. I think this is enough to show the point. If the evil is unknown (as we shall use in our example), then use black candles to represent this. If the evil is known to come from a specific direction, as, say, a single house, place your candles symbolizing the evil in the appropriate position (use your compass and a requisite map); then place your defensive candles accordingly on your altar, facing that direction. If it is felt to be all around, or the direction is unknown, then simply surround the Z/C of the person, as we show in our example.

Required:
Incense; Altar Candles; Z/C for the petitioner; four black candles, four red candles; four white candles.

Duration of the Ritual (maximum):
Nine consecutive days preferably, or nine consecutive Tuesdays (all in the hours of Mars).

A Ritual of Banishment in this particular case comes under the planet Mars, who is a martial, defensive, and fighting force, ruling (among other things) defence, soldiers, and war. Start on a Tuesday in the hour of Mars. Mark your candles into nine time periods (or mark one to use as a marker for the remainder). Light your incense of the planet. It should be a sharp, stimulating incense, even a little acrid. Light the Z/C for the petitioner: if you wish you can place a Z/C representing yourself and place it to 'stand by' the petitioner's Z/C. During the course of the ritual, name the petitioner, declaring your desire to assist him through this adverse period. Light the black candles, remembering to use a separate source for this, *not* the A/C. Do not use the black candles to light anything else unless it is evil, destructive, etc. Contemplate their malignant, destructive light for a while, attempting to visualise the evil depressive forces at work in the petitioner's life and the results that have finally brought him/her to you to ask for assistance. Then invoke the Angel Samael, Angel of the

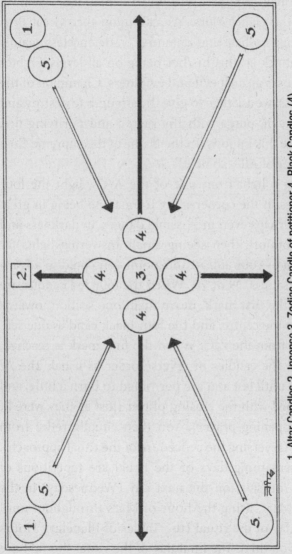

1. Altar Candles 2. Incense 3. Zodiac Candle of petitioner 4. Black Candles (4)
5. Red Candles (4) 6. White Candles (4: optional – see text)

Figure 6

planet Mars, to come to your aid to assist you in this matter. Your Invocation may be along the lines: 'Lord Samael, Angel of the planet Mars. We call upon thee Great Protective Angel to help and defend . . . , defenceless against this evil attack against his/her being on all levels. Fighter in Just Causes against evil and evildoers, Champion of the Defenceless, we ask thee to give thy strength to destroy and abate this evil, purge with thy sacred and purifying fire, and cleanse this iniquity. In the Name of the Supreme Cosmic Creator of All – so be it!'

Taking a light from one of the A/Cs, light the four red candles in the corners. Try to imagine being in great trouble, perhaps even in possible danger, in darkness and without comfort, then seeing small answering lights far off coming to your aid. At this point you could to advantage use Psalm 3, 59 or 70. When the four red candles are almost to the first mark, move them one section towards the Z/C in the centre, and the four black candles one section away from the Z/C. When the first mark is reached, extinguish the candles in reverse order as usual. The A/Cs are left until last and are permitted to burn a little, and extinguished with the closing prayer (just as they were lit with the opening prayer). You then ritually retire from your altar (reversing the procedure of the ritual approach).

The remaining days of the ritual are repetitious of the first. You start on the next day (Wednesday) in the hours of Mars, using the hour of Mars throughout until the final day of the ritual (the Tables of Planetary Hours will give you this). The final day of the ritual should have the four red Candles of Protection around the Z/C of the petitioner, and the black candles either going out (or out) furthest away from the petitioner. About the seventh day, you can put your four white candles in the places occupied by the four black candles when the ritual began. Light them from one of the A/Cs, letting everything burn out naturally on the final day, and ritually closing as before.

If the assistance required was from people of power, authority, and position, then you would replace the red candles with orange candles (for the Sun). If it related to law, church, or university, then purple (Jupiter); if for the comfort of love and affection, marriage, or any kind of partnership, then blue or pink candles (Venus/Libra). Assistance may be sought for illness, perhaps a mental disharmony or nervous affliction, in which case you would bring yellow candles (Mercury) to the petitioner, and so forth. In every case remove the negative and destructive to bring about the positive and constructive. If a person is afflicted by enemies who are known *(be very sure of this or leave it out)*, they are represented by correct, negated Z/Cs, slowly moved away from the petitioner until the Candles of Protection are moved between the oppressor(s) and the oppressed. A person of deep religious conviction could enlarge upon this by using red and purple candles or red/purple ones, the 'red' for the protective angel and the 'purple' for the Church. For the 'protection of love,' use red and pink, or red/pink – the combinations are virtually endless. I am confident that once the basic concepts are understood the reader will find no difficulty in devising rituals for his own particular requirements.

Rituals of Peace and Contemplation (Figure 7)

The reader must never forget that rituals need not be performed only in times of trouble or stress. Rituals of Peace and Contemplation can be created, perhaps even an occasional one just to say 'thank you'! Quite often in these peaceful, free reveries, solutions to many problems present themselves without any apparent effort, when the lower mind is held in abeyance from its usual round of worrying, fretting, and idle chattering. Let us take a possible example of how such a ritual may operate.

Perform the ritual when you are moved to do it any hour or day, though naturally you may select both hour and day as you wish. Light your incense, and this time make it one of which you are particularly fond. Open the ritual in the customary manner and light your A/Cs. Light three white candles from one of the A/Cs, placing them in the form of a triangle for the Trinity, in the front centre of the altar, saying: 'In the name of God the Father/Mother (light the first), God the Son (light the second), and God the Holy Spirit, or Shekinah (light the last)'. These candles should be in the form of a 'V', with the lower point towards the front of the altar.

Next, light seven Angelic/Planetary Candles, one for each of the angels (take the colors from the Tables). Place them around the Trinity Candles in the form of a 'V' with the lower point to the front also. Light the single candle at the bottom of the 'V' first, the Mercury candle, then in zigzag fashion, to the Sun next right, over to the Moon, back right for Venus, left to Jupiter, right for Mars, and ending

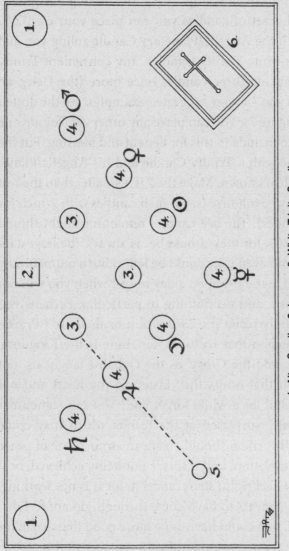

1. Altar Candles 2. Incense 3. White Trinity Candles
4. Angelic Candles (7) 5. Zodiac Candle 6. Bible (optional)

Figure 7

left, naturally, with Saturn. As you light each candle, thank each angel for his blessings – ask for nothing, try giving. Outside this set of candles you can place your own Z/C in line with the Angelic/Planetary Candle ruling you and one of the white Trinity Candles, any convenient Trinity Candle, making three candles once more (the Deity, an angel, and you – as per suggested examples: see the dotted lines on Figure 7). You can place any other Z/C for anyone you wish to include in this for benefit and blessing. Put the Z/C in line with a Trinity Candle and his Angelic/Planetary Candle if known. Make the Z/Cs smaller than the rest so that they go out first (say 5-inch candles with 7-inch for the remainder). The last candles remaining alight should be your A/Cs, for they should be, as always, the largest on the altar, and even they could be left to burn out naturally this time. Do the ritual on a day of rest when you will not be disturbed, and do nothing in particular. Perhaps you could usefully recite the 23rd Psalm or the Lord's Prayer. Use the version that includes 'for thine is the Kingdom, the Power, and the Glory' as the Qabalist taught us, not the version that omits this. Listen to the heart and not the head, and for a while forget 'me'! You can sometimes be pleasantly surprised at the results which may come through. This ritual should create an atmosphere of peace and contemplation, and if this is not being achieved, or if it does not 'feel right', then cancel it, for it is not working. If nothing appears to have 'come through', do not feel disappointed. You could have done more good than harm for the future; try it – you may like it.

Alternative Version (See Figure 8)

An alternative form which, as it uses rather a lot of candles, could be kept for those extra special occasions, uses only one A/C placed in the centre of the altar and not at the rear. Form three white candles into a triangle round the A/C. Around the Trinity Candles place seven Angelic/Planetary Candles in an evenly spaced circle (see Figure 8). Around this circle of seven, place twelve candles of the appropriate color to represent the twelve signs of the Zodiac, in strict Zodiacal order, naturally. They will not match up with the seven Planetary Candles, so do not try to do so. Place the first red candle for Aries at the left of the circle at the 9 o'clock position, Cancer at 6 o'clock, with Libra at 3 o'clock, and finally Capricorn at 12 o'clock, with the remainder of the candles correctly placed in color order between these four Cardinal Signs of the Zodiac. Check Figure 8.

This form of ritual has simple Qabalistic overtones in its uncomplicated design: the One is represented by the Altar Candle (the Deity) manifesting in the Three – the Trinity Candles (the Supernals); from the Three over the Abyss to the Seven – these, not counting the Deity of course, making the Ten (the Sephirah). It also represents the horoscope, the 'circle of your life' – the seven planets of old, the twelve signs of the Zodiac with the Trinity and Deity at the centre of the 'wheel' as the hub of your life – that which should support and hold it together.

This particular form of the ritual uses a large amount of candles, and it is perhaps kept for those 'once-a-year' occasions. The ritual has been given in its fullest form, which does not necessarily mean that it has to be used in this way. A section of it can be taken and used. You may choose to devise a ritual around the A/C and the three Trinity Candles, from the Ineffable Source of All to Its division into the Trinity of most religious philosophies. A second form could extend from the Trinity Candles to the seven Angelic or Planetary Candles. The addition of the twelve candles for the signs of the Zodiac at this point brings us back to the full form of the ritual once more. The complete form is an excellent ritual for group or school participation, the teacher or leader of the group supplying, say, the A/C, with perhaps the three most senior members or foundation members bringing one candle each for the Trinity. An ideal combination for this, if possible, is one male and two female, or one female and two male, each bringing and lighting a Trinity Candle. Seven people will bring an Angelic or Planetary Candle each; finally twelve people bring a colored candle (one for each Sign of the Zodiac) and, preferably, a son or daughter born under that particular Sign. All in the group bring their own personal Zodiac Candle, which are placed in their correct positions around the circles. It is obvious that if the group is small there will have to be duplication of people; but more important than this is that the correct number of candles are brought to the altar – one, then three; seven, then twelve. The possibilities of building up a group ritual around this are boundless if carefully devised. The potential for welding a group of people together is tremendous.

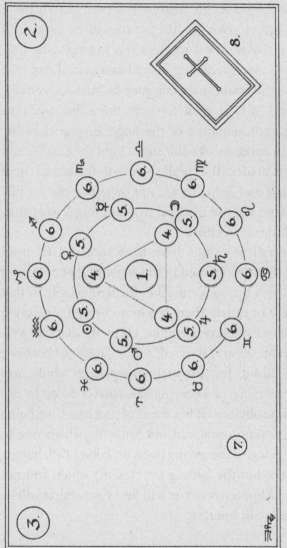

1. Altar Candle 2. Incense 3. Salt water 4. White Trinity Candles 5. Planetary Candles
6. Zodiac Candles (12) 7. Zodiac Candle (optional) 8. Bible (optional)

Figure 8

Emergency Rituals

Throughout the book, great stress has been placed upon using the correct color for the candles to be used, and this heading shows how important it is to emphasise this. Quite often in an emergency, an elaborate ritual can take too long, or the emotional state may be such as to make it impractical. It is at such times as these that you take one candle, representative of the angel or planet ruling the matter in hand, invoke the angel, light the candle, and stand it in its holder. That is all there is to the actual ritual for invocation and help. This is *not carte-blanche* for idle people to avoid the use of ritual in order to get what they want with little or no effort.

Many excellent results have been recorded from an emergency ritual performed in the white heat of crisis and emergency with the concentration focused acutely in that brief moment of ritual. There is a lot to be said for having seven Angelic/Planetary Candles, correctly marked with Angelic Signatures and dressed, tucked away somewhere, like a 'first-aid kit,' for just such emergencies which may arise. The necessity of knowing the correct color to use should now be obvious. It is a waste of precious time being faced with 'seven doors' and not knowing which one to enter, or in going to the wrong door, or worst of all, having the right door but the 'wrong key' (color) which will not fit. So do your homework; you will find your efforts will be compensated with interest.

The Magical or Mystical Novena

The Roman Catholic Church granted an indulgence when penitence was shown, a remission of temporal penalties for sin. The mediaeval view is set out in the bull, *'Unigenitus'* of Clement VI in 1343. The indulgence was granted on condition of certain acts by the indulged (contributions for the building of churches and so forth). Later, during the sixteenth century, there were considerable abuses, such as the sale of indulgences by professional 'pardoners,' whose false doctrine and scandalous conduct were an immediate occasion of the Reformation, and whose activities were finally abolished by Pius V in 1567.

The theory of indulgences in the Roman Catholic Church seems to be founded on three basic conditions. 1. That there is, even after penitence, retribution for sin either on earth or in purgatory. 2. That there is a 'treasury of merit,' that is, the infinite merits of Christ, with the merits of the Blessed Virgin Mary and saints available to the church by virtue of the Communion of the Saints. 3. The belief that the Church, by her powers of jurisdiction, has access and right of administration of merits in consideration of prayers, pious works, or other offerings of the faithful. One of the 'pious works' for which an indulgence was sometimes granted was the performance of a *novena*.

The novena used in the Church is a period of nine days of public or private devotion, by which it is hoped to obtain some special grace (Latin: *novena* – nine: *novenarius* – 'of nine days'). The general observation of novenas is relatively modern, dating as it does from the seventeenth century, though it is modelled on the nine days of preparation of the Apostles and Mary for the descent of the Spirit at Pentecost (Whitsunday: see Acts 1:13 and 2:1). There are other instances which feature nine days of preparation. Novenas may be arranged either in circumstances of special peril or need, or as a recurring devotional.

Obviously we are not going to use the Church novena, which is why this section is headed 'The Magical or Mystical Novena.' We will even continue to use the word 'novena' despite the fact that nine is not being used as the basic number or unit, but the mystical, magical seven, which, as far as this writer is concerned, is the only one to use when this ritual is used magically by those following the occult path. We use the Seven Planets of old and their angels. These are often considered the 'Seven Spirits before the Throne,' which God set in the heavens to watch over the earth, 'which are the Seven Spirits of God sent forth into all the earth' (Revelation 5:6). Modern astrology uses ten planets. In this section we only use seven. Starting with the appropriate planet and angel according to the purpose of the novena (of which more later), you add the Power of the Seven Angels in a cumulative effect, thus strengthening your invocation or petition, and building up the power by steadily maintained invocation or prayer.

The concept of constant, concentrated ritual or prayer is not new and is fundamental to most religious philosophies. The Taoist of the Middle Way would say it is like the gentle, but persistent drip of water that wears away the rock, or the grass that pushes itself ever upwards through seemingly unyielding materials. Your novena need not last seven days, however, unless you wish it to do so, although it should last seven hours at least, or seven times seven at most (that is, forty-nine hours, just over two days). In using the septenary, each of the angels is invoked in sequence and no one is omitted. A sequence consisting of less or more than seven destroys this sacred order. The novena should be regarded as something special and not used for any matter that may be deemed trivial; save it for circumstances of 'special peril and need,' not for something that could be solved by a little thought, ingenuity, hard work, and perhaps some inconvenience on your part.

Some occult writers point out that Christian practices, especially those of the Catholic persuasion, weaken the effectiveness of their novena by praying to their saints and *not* to the angels directly. Whilst preferring the angelic naturally, I have always felt that this criticism, properly viewed, is a rather sweeping and somewhat unfair one. The use of a religious symbol, such as the figure of a saint, to focus and concentrate the mind or prayer is a useful adjunct to both prayer and ritual – provided it is regarded and used as a prayer or invocation to the power *behind* the symbol and *not to* the symbol itself.

To start your novena, you have to decide what you are to petition for. As always, this requires very careful thought and a practical consideration of all the channels that are ordinarily available to you – it's not just a matter of 'I want'! If, however, you have tried all these outlets and resources, and the matter is *really* important to you, then you can start to think about your novena and make the relevant preparations. First, refer to the Tables (p. 107) from which you obtain the name of the angel who rules the matter in which you have interest. Then take the names of the planet and day and consult the Table of Planetary Hours, which will give you the hours available for use (you can start your novena in any of them). The Tables show that a planet and angel rule a certain day, and that there are certain hours during that day when both planet and angel are at their strongest (as for example the first hour of the day, which *always* belongs to the angel and planet which rules that day). Put simply, a good end depends on a good beginning. If you are trying to gain a favour from a person, the best way is to go and see him and present your request is when he is at home, not when he's out. Another very important point to remember is that a novena is used for one petition and *one petition only;* it is not a 'shopping-list,' so for this reason we are told to make our novena for important matters and not trivial ones.

You will have to decide before you begin how long your novena is going to last, and examples are given later. By looking at the Tables, you will see that there are seven planets, angels, days of the week, etc. (the other angels, planets, etc., are noted but are not used in this particular section). Therefore, the minimum sequence for a novena should be seven hours. You can extend this to fourteen, twenty-one, or further multiples of seven. The practical limit may prove to be the 'seven times seven' novena of forty-nine hours, just over two days. What of the nine-day novena which people in the past performed and from which it obtained its name? I personally would place an absolute limit of seven days (168 hours or 24 sequences of seven) when the mystical or magical novena is performed by those who follow the occult philosophy. I have seen this done by groups sharing the rota of work when all are agreed on its necessity. Can a novena be performed in more convenient sections? This *has* been done, and while nothing can replace the steady, continuous effectiveness of a novena performed without a break, I am sure that a *sincere* novena, performed in parts because of the responsibilities imposed by modern life, would not be unacceptable.

The secret of the novena, the *true* novena, is maintained pressure, *without any breaks*. Some teachers tell their students that they can perform one hour per day until the sequence chosen is completed, but if this is all the time you can spare I cannot see that your petition is important enough. However, if you decided on a 'seven by seven' novena and cannot perform it all in one go, then you can perform seven hours per day for seven days. This means you would pick up the correct hour for the angel and planet in the sequence on the following day. Let us say you are dedicating your novena to the Archangel Michael, Angel of the Sun. You will begin in an hour of the Sun on his day (Sunday). This would mean having to complete a full sequence of seven. You start the next sequence in the hour of the Sun and the Archangel Michael on Monday, completing the next sequence of seven angels. Do the same on Tuesday through to Saturday, when the novena will have been completed, each day starting in the hour of Archangel Michael, the Solar Angel.

If you look at the Tables we will illustrate this, using the Archangel Michael, taking a seven by seven novena. On Sunday you could start at 12 A.M. and finish at 7 A.M., or start at 7 A.M. and finish at 2 P.M., or at 2 P.M. and finish at 9 P.M., or finally, you can start at 9 P.M. and finish at 4 A.M. on Monday morning. You would then pick up the order on Monday, for the second sequence, starting again with the hour of the Sun, using 4 A.M. finishing 11 A.M., 11 A.M. finishing at 6 P.M., and finally starting at 6 P.M. and finishing at 1 A.M. on Tuesday morning. This crossing over into the next day is perfectly acceptable since the sequence was started on the correct day, Monday, and so on until the novena is finished on Saturday. It is most important to remember that during the novena none of the candles should be permitted to go out. The light of the first candle is transferred to the second, the second to the third, and so on until the novena is finished, *all* the candles being allowed to burn themselves out naturally. The candles must be fresh ones that have not been used for any other purpose, candles to which no light has been applied. You can use candles or nightlights. The only requirement is that the light used must last a minimum of one hour, preferably more, otherwise you will not be able to pass the flame to the next candle at the beginning of the next hour, for if the light of the last candle lit goes out before the flame has been passed on to the next candle, then the novena has been abortive and *must* be abandoned. You can use colored candles if you wish, or nightlights in colored containers. This would mean that you would have to have the sequence of colors according to the lists in the Tables, though white does just as well for a novena.

You may care to consider, or even use, my method of preparation for the novena. I use large decorative plates (I collect plates bearing relevant design, color, etc.) on which I set up my candles/nightlights, one in the centre for the angel petitioned by the novena, the remaining six lights spaced equally around the centre light. The candles are lit in a *clockwise* direction after the centre one (deosil – the same direction as the Sun), so they must be placed around the centre in this order. If I am going to carry on beyond the first seven sequences, I have another plate prepared so that I can transfer the light of the seventh candle to the first candle of the next sequence on the second plate. If you are using candles, usually two prepared plates are all that are needed. By the time the second plate is burnt out, you will have cleared and prepared the first plate in readiness for the third sequence, if you are going on. The use of this plate method is a fairly safe one. The plate contains the candle-wax, but it should stand on something that resists heat. You can use the same system equally well for nightlights, but as these burn much longer than candles (approximately 8 hours each), you will need many more plates and subsequently, more room, so I personally use candles, though the effect of the great number of nightlights lit is rather impressive. As you may well have a fair number of lights lit during the ritual of a novena, safety precautions to prevent fire should be a matter of common sense.

A personal variation is to put a colored candle *not* on the prepared plates but separated from them, of the appropriate color (Zodiac Candle) to represent myself or the person for whom the novena is being undertaken. After invoking and lighting the first candle of the novena, you take a light from that candle and light the personal Zodiac

Candle. You do this by taking your candle and lighting it from the Angel's Candle (the candle of the angel who rules the novena, the first one lit in *all* the sequences of seven), and with the request 'by your leave,' you light your candle from his. Do *not* use the same match to light both candles, *only* the Angelic Candle. In this you are symbolically requesting that the angel grant, and give you, one small spark of his light. This is only necessary once in order to form a 'link' with the angel for either yourself (the petitioner) or on behalf of the person for whom you are petitioning. If you wish to keep the Zodiac Candle burning throughout the novena (this is optional, but desirable in my view), light a new Zodiac Candle from the flame of the old one before it goes out, putting the new candle on top of the old. If the Zodiac Candle goes out at any time, do not abort the Ritual as mentioned before (only do that if the Angelic Candles go out), simply relight your Zodiac Candle as before and in the same manner.

Now let us take a 'dry-run' through a novena to see how it may be performed in actual practice. First, having decided on the necessity for the novena, we frame our petition or invocation – that which we are trying to achieve. Think very carefully on this. Next we look at the Tables to see which angel, planet, day of the week, etc., is the ruler of the matter. Let us say that we have exhausted all normal channels open to us and that we need help desperately in matters of property and estate. The Tables will show that these matters are under the jurisdiction of the Angel Cassiel and the planet Saturn, and give the colors and the angel's day (Saturday).

You next have to decide for how long you are going to perform your novena. Having decided, you next look down the Tables of Planetary Hours for Saturday and the hours of the planet Saturn and you will find you can start at 12 A.M., 7 A.M., 2 P.M., and 9 P.M. (or the 1st, 8th, 15th, and 22nd hour 'after sunrise' if you are using the alternative system). If you are performing only one sequence of seven, you have four periods in which it can be accomplished on that day. If you are doing a *continuous* 'seven times seven,' you will finish at 8 A.M. on Monday morning, if you commenced your novena at 7 A.M. on Saturday. If you are undertaking a 'seven times seven' but cannot do the continuous novena (so are undertaking seven hours per day for seven days), you can start in any of the four sequences on Saturday as given above. On Sunday you will start again in one of the hours of Saturn (in any novena of Saturn and the Angel Cassiel you start with Saturn and end with the Moon). On Sunday, you can use 4 A.M., 11 A.M., and 6 P.M. – three periods this time. You do the same on each day, and if you use the 11 P.M. sequence on Wednesday, it does not matter that it runs into Thursday, because it was *started* on Wednesday. Do not forget the Thursday sequence, thinking that because you have worked from Wednesday into Thursday that it has already been completed. Remember, one full sequence every day.

You would end this particular novena on Friday, the last septenary available on that day being 5 p.m. The 'Saturn Septenary' being Saturn, Jupiter, Mars, Sun, Venus, Mercury, and the Moon, the order of the planets is always maintained no matter which angel or planet you start with.

Once you have worked out the pattern of the first seven of the sequence you are using, the remaining sequences are identical if you are going on to more than one sequence of seven, so you prepare the required amount and order of the lights accordingly.

When you start lighting the first candle, do *not* light it as the clock actually strikes the hour, but pause a moment to enable the new hour to 'establish' itself and the change-over to be complete. Do likewise with all the remaining hours, or whenever time is involved in ritual. I have said elsewhere and it bears repetition, please *use matches*. The wood of the match was once part of a living entity; the action of 'striking' is still a symbolic act of 'living fire,' or 'new fire,' which has been 'called up' for the occasion.

Staying with the above example (Angel Cassiel/Planet Saturn/Saturday), when lighting your first candle/night-light, you could say something along the following lines: 'Lord [or Angel] Cassiel, Angel of Saturn, Ruler of this the day and hour of my novena, and to whom it is dedicated. Look with favour and grant thy blessings upon this novena, and my magical efforts to ... [at this point give brief details of the reason which has caused you to resort to a magical novena] ... which has eluded my efforts to bring it to fruition.' If you are using a Zodiac Candle (of the appropriate color), either for yourself, or the person on whose behalf you are petitioning, at this point make the request 'by your leave,' light it from the Angel's Candle, and say (in this example): 'Lord Cassiel, grant that a small spark from your aura may illumine my [or name the petitioner, if not you] mind and life, so that the darkness and ignorance may

be dispelled; that it may bring light to our problem, which we have appealed for thy help to resolve [or banish, etc.].'
As always I suggest that the above need not be slavishly copied; it is only given to propose the way a novena may be constructed. You can use your own words, from any source which has meaning, but I must stress, that it must have *meaning to you,* in *any* language.

The Archangel Raphael (planet Mercury) works quickly. He rules your mind and speech among other things, so he has helped you to formulate your petition. He knows it before you say it, but say it all the same! Angel Samael (planet Mars) hates 'waffle,' so be brief and to the point – 'flowery' orations will get you nowhere with him, but it may well succeed with the Angel Anael (planet Venus), who rules art and beautiful things. The Angel Sachiel (planet Jupiter) loves ceremony, ritual, pomp, and circumstance, so their use enhances any dealings with this angel, as it would with Archangel Michael, and so on for the remaining angels.

You can add the names of the subsequent angels to the angel first invoked and petitioned (the ruler of the novena), as their hours follow in one of two ways. You can simply petition the angel of the current hour to add his powers to the powers of the angel of the novena (in our example Jupiter follows Saturn, so you could use – 'Lord Sachiel, Angel of Jupiter, please look with favour upon my novena, and add thy powers and blessings to those of Lord Cassiel).' In the next hour you would substitute 'Lord Samael' (Angel of Mars) in the above text; in the next hour 'Lord Michael' (Archangel of the Sun), and so on.

An alternative form is to name the angels in full, until on the seventh hour you are naming all seven angels. In our example the seventh angel in the sequence would be the Archangel Gabriel, Angel of the Moon, so you request that he give his assistance to aid the other six. (For example, 'Lord Gabriel, I do petition thee to assist and bless my novena by adding your power to those of the Lords Cassiel, Sachiel, Samael, Michael, Anael, and Raphael, to aid my petition and bring this matter to a successful conclusion.') If you are doing more than one seven-hour series, you would start (with this alternative form) at the beginning again, with the first angel once more, and add each angel's name every hour until you are naming the full seven once more at the seventh hour, and so on.

At first a novena may appear very complicated, but it is not so really. Let us take a brief look at the main points once more. First, find out from the Tables which angel and planet rule the matter for which you are petitioning. You start your novena on the day and in the hour of the angel ruling the matter and for this you consult your Tables of Planetary Hours. The order of the planets in the Tables never changes; no matter what angel, planet, day, or hour you start, the sequence stays the same. The suggestions given elsewhere and explained regarding the phases of the Moon should be observed, if possible. If the novena is for acquisition, growth, and attraction, try to use a waxing Moon, or a Moon that is 'growing' (as indeed she appears to do physically) from New Moon to Full – the nearer to the date of the New Moon the better. If the results hoped for are for banishment, termination, or decrease, try to use the period from the Full Moon to the Last Quarter. It is best not to start a novena at the Full Moon unless it is unavoidable (though it is immaterial that it may occur *during* the course of the novena). Never begin during the period called 'the Dark of the Moon,' three days before the date of the New Moon.

Finally, what should *you* do during your novena? This depends so much on personal temperament that it cannot really be legislated for. There are those with 'wills of iron' permitting almost total concentration on the work in hand, but there will be a greater number who will not achieve this, and perhaps would not wish to. I personally prepare light food and drinks, stay in the room in which the novena is being observed as much as possible, and undertake to create as relaxed and contemplative an atmosphere as possible (using low volume music of appropriate mood) by putting my life into 'low gear.'

Some References to the Psalms

One of the most fruitful sources of material for the construction of rituals is the Biblical Psalms. The reader would do well in any free moments to reread these verses with fresh eyes and a new perspective. It is not by any means the first time they have been used for this purpose, as the *Sepher Schimmush Tehillim* (or 'Use of Psalms for the physical welfare of Man,' published in 1788 and translated by Godfrey Selig) attests. The following list contains suggestions taken from long usage in ritual. They should give enough examples to set the reader on the right lines and encourage their future use. In the above work we are told: 'Yes, dear reader you must not doubt. Through pious life and by rational use of the Psalms you may obtain the grace of God, the favour of princes and magistrates and the love of your fellow-men. You will be able to protect yourself from danger, to escape suffering, and to promote your own welfare.'

For defence against enemies, assailants, and rivals: Pss. 3; 59; 70.
For illness and/or bad health: Pss. 35; 38.
For recovery from illness or thanksgiving: Ps. 30.
For support in times of stress or affliction: Pss. 3; 25; 54.
To bring peace and/or blessings to the home: Pss. l; 128.
For anyone under evil conditions or duress: Pss. 71; 93.
For conditions that cause a person fear: Ps. 31.
For protection of self and others in a dangerous situation: Pss. 35; 36.
For bringing unity between people or groups: Ps. 133.
To petition material comforts, money, food, and so forth: Ps. 41.
Supplication: Ps. 131.
For receiving grace, love, and mercy: Ps. 32.
For opening a ritual: Pss. 130; 134.
For trouble with anxiety of a restless conscience or heavy sin: Ps. 51.
For trouble by slander or calumny: Pss. 38; 39.
For safety in evil, evil situations, etc.: Pss. 30; 121.
For use of learned men, especially students before entering college: Ps. 134.
For a happy escape from great danger, or having received particular grace from the Lord of Hosts: Ps. 150.

In matters of love and the affections, a favourite is the Song of Solomon, which can prove most useful. Take

Chapter 6 if the petitioner is male, and Chapter 18 if female. It is further given to us from an old manuscript that whosoever prays the following five verses daily and hourly to God 'will have propriety and blessings in all his undertakings.' The verses must be spoken in the following order; Ps. 121 verse 2; Ps. 55 verse 23; Ps. 37 verse 37; Ps. 36 verse 3; Ps. 143 verse 13.

Finally, can the whole subject of candle magic, in its essence so to speak, be put in a nutshell? Yes, I think it can, but not by me. I must make use of words in the work of a great Master to accomplish this. In a tale by his hand we have two companions returning home: 'That light we see is burning in my hall. How far that little candle throws his beams! So shines a good deed in a naughty world.' Her companion replies: 'When the moon shone, we did not see the candle.' She answers: 'So doth the greater glory dim the less: A substitute shines brightly as a king until a king be by, and then his state empties itself, as doth an inland brook into the main of waters.'

The rituals you perform in all sincerity can be likened to that 'little candle' shining 'like a good deed in a naughty world.' The candles you place on your Altar of Light, when lit in Angelic Invocation, shine 'brightly as a king until a king be by.' Angelic Beings of Pure Light such as not seen here on earth *may* empty themselves like 'an inland brook into the main of waters,' which is *your altar,* and bestow their blessings and grace upon the practitioner and his good works.

REFERENCE TABLES

Dates for the Signs of the Zodiac and the Zodiac Colors

The dates below give the dates of the Sun's entry into the twelve Signs of the Zodiac. These are, in general, accurate enough, and although there is a slight variation it should not be sufficient to make them unacceptable. The only people whom this may affect are those born on the actual day of the change. If this is so, an ephemeris for the year of birth may be needed to confirm the true Sign of the Zodiac.

21 March–20 April
Sign: ARIES. Ruling Planet: MARS.
Colors: Bright reds, scarlet, and crimson, the brightest and most 'full-blooded,' no dull colors.

21 April–21 May
Sign: TAURUS. Ruling Planet: VENUS.
Colors: Bright greens, apple green, olive green, none of the dark colors but fresh and vibrant, as 'Nature' is in the 'growth' of Spring.

22 May–21 June
Sign: GEMINI. Ruling Planet: MERCURY.

Colors: Bright yellow, occasionally orange (preferably a bright one).

22 June–22 July
Sign: CANCER. Ruling Planet: MOON.
Colors: White, silver, mother-of-pearl. Alternatives are the palest of green, blue, and sometimes mauve.

23 July–23 August
Sign: LEO. Ruling Planet: SUN.
Colors: Gold, orange, gilt, occasionally yellow (preferably a dark one).

24 August–23 September
Sign: VIRGO. Ruling Planet: MERCURY.
Colors: Light and golden browns, warm and rich. Midgreens, russets, colors generally accepted as 'autumnal,' as Nature is when preparing for winter.

24 September–23 October
Sign: LIBRA. Ruling Planet: VENUS.
Colors: Pink, rose pink, and royal blue (bright).

24 October–22 November
Sign: SCORPIO. Ruling Planet: MARS. Sub-ruler: PLUTO.
Colors: Dark reds and crimsons (the darker the better). Silver grey and black (do not use black in candles; see note below).

23 November–21 December

Sign: SAGITTARIUS. Ruling Planet: JUPITER.

Colors: Purple, mauve, lavender. Royal or dark blue occasionally; use only if the other colors are not available.

22 December–20 January

Sign: CAPRICORN. Ruling Planet: SATURN.

Colors: Darkest greens, like the 'evergreens' that keep their foliage during the winter months. Dark brown and greys. Black (do not use black in candles; see note below).

21 January–19 February

Sign: AQUARIUS. Ruling Planet: SATURN. Sub-ruler: URANUS.

Colors: (Mainly Uranus.) Electric blue, multi-colored hues, bright plaid colors, and mixtures. 'Shot-silk' effects or any startling combinations of color, such as fluorescent. Use Capricorn for the colors of Saturn.

20 February–20 March

SignPISCES. Ruling Planet: JUPITER. Sub-ruler: NEPTUNE.

Colors: (Mainly Neptune.) Sea-greens, palest mauve and lavender, iridescent and shimmering colors or colors that 'appear to be what they are not' – 'illusory.' Use Sagittarius for the colors of Jupiter.

The reader will note that three of the signs have two planets as rulers; this is because modern astrology has allocated these recent planets as the new rulers, taking over from the older, traditional ones, which many people do not use, though they do accept the modern rulers as sub-rulers or co-rulers. The seven planets of old, save the Sun and Moon, have two modes or channels of expression: male/female, positive/negative, and so forth, both equal in power and status. Use of the modern planets removes one of these modes of expression. Some practitioners cannot, or do not, use them as rulers because of this, regarding them as co-rulers in use, acknowledgment, and consideration. This is something that the reader, either now or later, will have to resolve for himself as his knowledge and experience grow; either to follow the old and acknowledge the new, or to completely abandon the old in favour of the new. At all times, however, both rulers are given.

Some of the Signs of the Zodiac have black as one of the colors for both sign and planet (see Scorpio and Capricorn), but because of the special way *black candles* are used and regarded in candle rituals it is considered that this is best avoided and the alternatives used, so please avoid the use of black unless it is in the manner prescribed in the text.

Days of the Week/Zodiac Signs/Ruling Planets/Angelic Rulerships/Matters Ruled

In the lists that follow, by reasons in part of the dual rulerships, do not be surprised to find some duplication under other planets of certain matters. Both are acceptable; use either as you prefer. Likewise, some matters are at home with more than one planet because of the complex interplanetary relationships, especially if the lists contain, as these do, the attributes of signs of the zodiac and considerations of the natural horoscope houses, which have rulership over people and their affairs. The lists are by no means complete and the reader is expected to make his own additions to them.

Day of the Week: SUNDAY
Planetary ruler: SUN
Angel: ARCHANGEL MICHAEL or MIKAEL
Sign of the Zodiac: LEO

Matters of: Ambition; career; exaltation; honour; all masculine matters (with Mars); the heart (the physical organ); cardiac conditions; the chest and spine; fame and fortune; gold; magistrates; rank; royalty (with Jupiter); the sovereign (ruler and coin); people in high position and authority; the government; privy council; pedigree and 'breeding' (men and animals); the father or the head of groups and organizations; the human body (as a complete organism); health and healing; children; speculation; speculators and risk; diamonds; lovers (Venus rules 'love'); entertainers and entertainment; the theatre and the stage; actors; places of amusement; authority (used and misused); the despot and tyrant; pride and its 'fall'; arrogance and conceit; the letter of the Law.

Day of the Week: MONDAY
Planetary ruler: MOON
Angel: ARCHANGEL GABRIEL
Sign of the Zodiac: CANCER

Matters of: Women and the feminine; conception and fertility; development of psychic abilities; intuition; dealings with the public at large and the masses; change; rhythm and vacillation; the family; domesticity and the domestic; the mother; motherhood; obstetrics; babes and infants; the nursery and nursing; sleep; germination (of the night, womb, soil, etc.); nutrition, food, and the stomach; the breasts; emotion and weakness; the tides (the Moon rules not only the actual tides of the sea, but the 'tides' in many mundane and occult matters); water; the seas, ships, and mariners; the functioning of the body as a whole; inheritance; property and property with water, as with wells and streams, etc.; the home; anything that encloses and protects; lost things; candles.

Day of the Week: TUESDAY
Planetary ruler: MARS
Sub-ruler: PLUTO
Angel(s): ANGEL SAMAEL (for Aries/Mars);
    ANGEL AZRAEL (for Scorpio/Pluto)
Signs of the Zodiac: ARIES and SCORPIO
    N. B. All the following is subdivided between the angels given above, as will be the other signs that have relinquished one of their modes of expression to a later planet.

Angel Samael (Aries/Mars)
Matters of: Courage; daring and defiance; protection from danger on both the physical and other planes; protection from danger and peril (especially fire); machinery,

in particular engineering; cutting tools, swords, daggers, knives, etc.; adventure and misadventure; energy; cars and the internal combustion engine; war and its weapons (conventional, not gases or nuclear); battles and battlefields (the 'domestic' also); healthy, hale, and hearty; operations, surgery, and surgeons; the blood and bloodshed; pain; fevers; the 'physical' in most of its aspects; ability in leadership; ambition and the capacity to surmount obstacles and win; enterprise; words that 'cut' as with sarcasm and criticism; new ventures; accidents, especially burning, scalding, and cuts; newcomers; arrivals; self-interest; headlong, headstrong, and headfirst; violence; uncontrolled outbursts (as with temper).

Angel Azrael (Scorpio/Pluto)

Matters of: The 'underworld' (of the dead and the criminal); the 'afterlife'; things that are hidden and out of sight; buried in the depths of your mind (the subconscious), or in the earth (as with oils, gases, precious stones and minerals, etc.); secret and subversive people and enemies; the 'bringing to light' of matters; regeneration; recuperation; transmutation; the dead and death; enlightenment (slow); scheming; metamorphosis; overthrow; the breaking up of the old to make way for the new (slowly, not like Uranus, who is quick and violent at times); relentlessness; evolution and revolution; fanaticism and fanatical people; pall-bearers; coroner; undertaker (mortician); surgeon (with Mars); debt and debt collectors; taxation and tax collectors; wills and legacies; losses and bankruptcy; 'afterlife' research.

Day of the Week: WEDNESDAY
Planetary ruler: MERCURY
Angel: ARCHANGEL RAPHAEL
Signs of the Zodiac: GEMINI and VIRGO

Matters of: Intellect; the mind, especially that part that deals with 'everyday' affairs, manual dexterity, etc.; writing, scripts, and alphabets; languages and their acquisition; all the tools of writing – pens and pencils; typewriters (mechanical with Mars); writing (letters, notes, books, etc.); the mental processes and perception; communication (mental and transport); the post and the postman; correspondence; newspapers and magazines; the telegraph and telegrams, etc.; rumours and reports; reporters; the acquisition of knowledge and skills; schools and education; skills that involve manual dexterity; power of reasoning; books, deeds, documents, certificates, anything that is written or printed; brothers and sisters; relatives (to a large extent); your immediate neighbourhood and neighbours; visits and visitors; your nervous system and 'nerves'; theft and thieves; breath and breathing, your lungs and their disorders; youth (yours) and youth in general; news; reports and information; messages and messengers; teachers; gossips; tenants; tradesmen; lodgers; sickness; disease and distress.

Day of the week: THURSDAY
Planetary ruler: JUPITER
Sub-ruler: NEPTUNE
Angels: ANGEL SACHIEL (for Sagittarius/Jupiter);
    ANGEL ASARIEL (for Pisces/Neptune)
Signs of the Zodiac: SAGITTARIUS and PISCES

Angel Sachiel (Sagittarius/Jupiter)

Matters of: Finance; banks; bankers and banking; prestige and social prominence; gambling, gamblers, and games of chance where bets are placed; horses, thoroughbred racehorses in particular, racecourses; luck in general; religions and philosophies; barristers and lawyers; the Law, of group, tribe, clan, nation, or country; legal and illegal; illicit; lawsuits; the church and its dignitaries (all denominations); universities; higher and advanced education; profit and expansion; embezzlement; stocks and shares; the Stock Exchange; the Treasury; wealth and the wealthy; Court (royal); the courts (legal); wisdom; publication and publishers; strangers and aliens; explorers; insurance and insurance investigators; grandchildren; places remote from the place of birth; dreams; foreign interests; ceremonies, rituals, and parades; the liver and blood, also their disorders.

Angel Asariel (Pisces/Neptune)

Matters of: Clairvoyance (passive); people and matters connected with the sea; mediums and the mediumistic; the 'astral'; crystal ball (these last two with the Moon); spirit and spiritualism; the mysterious, the unknown, and the unexplained; prophets and prophecy; psychic trance and catalepsy; vague, intangible, and dreamlike; elusive; incorporeal; inspiration; idealism; addicts and addiction (smoking, drinking, and drugs); artificial and synthetic, especially things that appear to be what they are not, illusory; imitation; fakes and forgeries (people as well as things); aliases; those who attack from ambush (as with friends whom you trust); 'self-undoing'; clandestine meetings, associations, and matters; secrets; recluses and hermits; informers; sacrifice and sacrificial; exile; detention; hospitals; asylums and prisons; bribery and corruption; secret sorrows; charitable work without recognition; suicide; 'fog and night'; that which films and veils.

Day of the Week: **FRIDAY**
Planetary ruler: **VENUS**
Angel: **ANGEL ANAEL**
Signs of the Zodiac: **TAURUS and LIBRA**

Matters of: Love; marriage, and partnership of all kinds; beauty; art; artists and the artistic; musical events and musicians (music proper is ruled by the Sun); social events, affairs, or gatherings; sociability; romance and courtship; weddings; wedding gowns and bouquets; elegance; harmony in all its aspects; pleasure; war and declared enemies and opponents; lust, lewdness, and licence; peace and peaceful imbalance; money (with Jupiter); your banker; investors and investments; the moveable possessions (those you take with you when you move, unlike your house); contracts and agreements; settlements; nieces and nephews; lawyers (barristers under Jupiter); the kidneys and their disorders.

Day of the Week: **SATURDAY**
Planetary ruler: **SATURN**
Sub-ruler: **URANUS**
Angels: **ANGEL CASSIEL (for Capricorn/Saturn);**
    ANGEL URIEL (for Aquarius/Uranus)
Signs of the Zodiac: **CAPRICORN and AQUARIUS**

Angel Cassiel (Capricorn/Saturn)

Matters of: Houses, property, and estate; old people and matters of long standing; old things; Karma; excavations; pits and mines (not necessarily what comes out of them); death as 'The Reaper'; the grave, vault, or sepulchre; Time itself as 'Father Time'; clocks and watches, instruments that measure time; punctuality; patience; endurance; stability; the wisdom that can be brought by age; self-discipline; age, aging, and the aged; debts that are owing, as with duty, money, obligations, and Karma; responsibility; depression; desolation; duty; economy; method and the methodical; thrift; 'the past'; sadness, mourning, grief, and loss; anything that impedes or obstructs; the 'immovable object' (Saturn) can be moved only by the 'irresistible force' (Uranus); when these two meet, 'something's got to give'; the career; your standing in the world outside the home, fame, and notoriety; famous and infamous; reputation; Fate; employer and employment; the Government; rheumatism (or illness brought about by cold, damp, or age).

Archangel Uriel (Aquarius/Uranus)

Matters of: Magical forces; sudden change (the 'Lightningstruck Tower'); the 'eleventh hour miracle' – in the nick of time; new, modern, and novel matters and inventions; liberty and license; paradox; inventors and inventions, especially electrical; nuclear and space technology, rockets, flights, etc.; chaos and crisis; divorce and separation; the occult and occultists; prophetic; pioneering; science and the scientific; the unconventional; nonconformity; the rebel – 'I won't!'; unpredictable (people, actions, things); enlightenment (sudden, 'a road to Damascus'); fanaticism; mutiny and mutineers; anarchy and anarchists; strikes (labour); magic and magicians (not the stage variety, which is illusion and Neptune – rather those who attempt to change or control their lives using natural forces, or otherwise, subjected to training of the willpower); the 'irresistible force'; hopes and wishes; humanitarian; friends; club members and unbonded relationships; fraternal; clubs, associations, and societies (not necessarily social); daughter- or son-in-law; miscarriage; deaths in the family.

Combining the lists throughout the work, you should be able to discover the rulership, color, angelic and planetary rulership, day of the week, and so forth, to represent most situations, emotions, and circumstances. If the situation requires news or information in a particular matter, this belongs to the sphere of the planet Mercury and its Archangel, Raphael, and this information you take from your lists. If it is to do with people of authority, use the Sun, or in some cases, Jupiter. If it is for information or news of these people, you could combine two colors, either on one candle or use two candles to represent the twin aspects of the question – e.g., yellow for news with purple or orange for authority. Pair these together in a twin candlestick, or keep the two colored candles next to each other and move them together throughout the Ritual to show that this is so. If it is loss, sadness, depression, or perhaps bereavement, then use the planet Saturn alone, a dark green candle. If an artistic person decided to invoke for increased imagination or inspiration to assist him in his work, the 'artistic' would fall within the sphere of the planet Venus, while the 'inspiration' would fall under either the Moon or Neptune. Problems relating to property and real estate, or housing generally, are Saturnian in nature, while courage and initiative are Martian. For ambition and career, your standing in the world, you can use the Sun, especially if you want 'to shine' in your given field. As you can see, the combinations are virtually endless. Quite often, reducing your problem down to its simple elements helps to get to the root or core of the problem and makes it easier to handle.

I have not given many examples of the negative aspects, as these are obvious enough from the given lists. For example, love degenerating into lust and sensuality; generosity into an embarrassing exhibition of over-indulgence or 'buying' your friends; practical and commendable economy into obsessive meanness and selfishness; harmony and accord into a seeking of 'peace at any price'; justice with mercy (compassion) into a pitiless seeking of justice without mercy (revenge). I do not feel it is necessary to give further examples. The above is so straightforward, as are the principles involved. I can, I am sure, safely leave it in the hands of the reader to devise his own alternatives, making additional lists for his own personal use.

Tables of Planetary Hours

'To everything there is a season, and a time to every purpose under the heaven.'

Ecclesiastes

One of the most important things that the Ancients stressed in most of their writings was the above sentiment, or something very similar. To find the correct time for all operations occupied a great deal of their labours, and not without justification. A great deal of occult or magical practice cannot be divorced from astrology in one form or another. Traditionally, it was necessary to perform your rituals or invocations, begin making or consecrating your talismans, make your incense, manufacture your Planetary/ Angelic Candles or candle rituals at certain times which were valid or effective for the purpose which you intended, otherwise it was pointless to make the effort at all.

As has been shown, amongst other things, the planets have dominion over certain days. Further, they have dominion over certain hours within each day. They also have subrulership over certain hours in days ruled by other planets, so giving a fairly wide choice with regard to the times you can select to perform your occult tasks.

The best method of all is to select the day that is ruled by the planet itself, for he is 'Lord of the Day', and on that day his influence is the strongest, for it 'vibrates' to him. His influence and power can be made even greater on his day by selecting the hours during that day over which he has personal rulership. If you are unable to use that day and his hours, then you could use the hours he sub-ruled in the day of another planet. Thus if you were doing a solar ritual, or any matter under the Sun's domain, you would pick the best day for that ritual, which is of course the day ruled by the Sun – Sunday. If you turn to the Tables on pp. 135–136, you will see that the Sun, under the column headed 'Sunday', rules the 1st, 8th, 15th, and 22nd hour 'after sunrise' on that day or, according to the column on the far right of the page, the hours, 12-1 A.M., 7-8 A.M., 2-3 P.M. and 9-10 P.M., according to which of the two systems available you decide to use.

The counsel of perfection would be to do the work of the planetary ruler of the operation *only* in the hours of that planet and on the actual day on which the planet rules. If you are unable to do this, then you work in the hours of the planet that are sub-ruled by him on the other days of the week.

When these tables were originally compiled, life went at a very different pace from that experienced today. These requirements could be satisfied within the ordered regimen of temple life by the priesthood, who could practise the art to its fullest, able as they were to devote their lives and all their waking hours to its perfection. However, do not let this discourage you – the main thing to remember in all this is *to start at the correct time*. If you cannot, or will not, do this then you are just wasting your efforts. A good analogy is growing plants from seed. By finding out, with the use of the table, the best time to plant your 'seeds', you are trying to ensure that the ones you do plant will grow and flourish, and that you will reap the 'harvest' you are hoping for. This does not mean that you cannot complete the task you have begun if it goes beyond the hour of the planet ruling the matter and into the next. After all, any person born between approximately 21/22 December to 19/20 January we call a 'Capricorn.' He keeps this 'birth-mark' throughout his entire life, because his entry into the physical was 'marked' by this time, along with the other various positions of the planets in the horoscope. In the same way, the task you begin will bear the 'mark' of the time in which you begin it.

Before we go any further, let us take a look at the two methods of using the Table of Planetary Hours. Ignore the two columns at either end for the moment. You will see between these two columns the headings of the seven days of the week from Sunday through to Saturday. Underneath each of these days of the week you will find a list of the seven planets used, one planet for each of the twenty-four hours of the day. These columns apply whichever time system you use, though the final decision must be yours.

The first hour is always of the planet which rules the day, and this applies to both systems. The reader will find some tables not starting this way, and this is the main reason why I disagree with them. Sunday is ruled by the Sun, Monday the Moon, Tuesday by Mars, Wednesday by Mercury, Thursday by Jupiter, Friday by Venus, and Saturday by Saturn. If, for instance, you were making a Ritual or Invocation to Mars (or *any* work of Mars), then you would do this on Tuesday, as Mars is the ruler of this day.

Let us look at the two systems used for this table. Both have their advocates, and I do not intend complicating the issue by stating a preference; I think it is far better that you make up your own mind. The one thing I stress is this: having decided which of the two you prefer to use, stick to it. Do not swap and change them around with whim and fancy, for it will only cause confusion on all levels. I do *not* mean, however, that your decision must be irrevocable. For if, in the light of experience, you wish to change it at a later date, then of course you can. The first system consists of simply using the column on the far right. This gives the hours of the day from midnight to noon, and back to midnight the next day, when the new day takes over. There is no need for any working out with this system. It simply follows the hours as marked out on the face of any clock. You completely ignore the column on the far left marked 'After Sunrise', taking the clock times as given on the far right.

Let us take an example to illustrate both systems so that they may be compared. If you are working with the planet Mercury, you would use the day he rules as your first choice of time, which is Wednesday. The best times to use that day are, naturally, the hours ruled by the planet itself, which are: the first hour of the day (always ruled by the planet ruling the day), which is 12-1 a.m., next, 7-8 a.m., next, 2-3 p.m., and finally 9-10 p.m. It may be that you cannot use that day for your work for one reason or another, and that Sunday is more convenient, so let us take a look at the best times for any work of Mercury on that day. If we go down the column for Sunday we find that the first hour ruled by Mercury is 2-3 a.m.; the next is 9-10 a.m.; then 4-5 p.m., and finally 11-12 p.m. (midnight). As you will see, you have four hours that you can use on Sunday. You follow this through for any other day that you want to use for convenience of working.

Do remember that starting at the right time is the most important rule of this chapter. You can work on the matter in hand until you finish it, no matter how long it takes, *provided* you have started in the correct hour ruled by the planet you are working under. If you can work only in the day and actual hours of the planet, so much the better; but if not, make the correct start and all will be well.

The one thing you will have to watch in either system is British Summer Time, or B.S.T., which usually comes into force around the middle of March and lasts to about the middle of October. During this period *all* clocks are advanced one hour. This must be taken into account when you are using this table, which, like most astrological tables, is given in Greenwich Mean Time (G.M.T.). Let us go back to our example of Mercury once more. When you are doing any work in the months when B.S.T. is in operation, one hour will have to be added to the times given in the table. Still using Mercury, the first hour of the day, 12-1 A.M., is now 1-2 A.M., because the clock is one hour *in advance* of G.M.T., while his other hours during this period will also have one hour added thus: 7-8 A.M. becomes 8-9 A.M.; 2-3 P.M. becomes 3-4 P.M.; and 9-10 P.M. becomes 10-11 P.M. Naturally, when the clocks have *not* been advanced one hour by B.S.T., or when B.S.T. is finished, you employ the times given on the right-hand side, which are *all* in G.M.T. A person working in a country operating Zone Times or Daylight Saving Times will have to make appropriate adjustments to convert the table, if necessary. The use of the second system appears at first sight more complicated. Although it does require a little more working out, it is really quite simple and should present no difficulty. In this system, we ignore the column on the far right, the 'clock times,' and take the column on the far left marked 'After Sunrise.' Under this heading you will find a list of numbers which represents the number of hours *after* sunrise. Thus, 1st represents the first hour after sunrise, 12th denotes the twelfth hour after sunrise, the 15th is the fifteenth hour after, and so on. This system is based upon the philosophy that the *true day* has not begun while the Sun is below the horizon, and that the day has only commenced when the 'Lord of the Day,' which is the Sun, has risen above the horizon and is shedding his light.

It is argued that although it is now generally accepted that the new day begins at midnight, this only came into being with the advent of machines to measure time. Prior to this, all work was done in the past in accordance with the movement of the heavenly bodies. The arrival of the Sun, naturally, heralded the start of the new day, giving short days in the winter and longer ones during the summer months. It cannot be claimed that midnight is the first hour of a new day when your eyes tell you it is plainly the middle of the night! If you find this concept preferable to the first system given, then this second system is the one to use, as it is based upon, and fits, this philosophy. If sunrise, let us say, is 6 A.M. in the area you are working, the 1st hour 'after sunrise' would be 6-7 A.M., the 2nd 7-8 A.M., the 3rd 8-9 A.M., and so on. Sunrise is not a constant thing; nor does it occur everywhere on earth at the same time. It is also seasonal, rising early in the summer months, and rising late and setting early in the winter. At midnight in England it is early afternoon or evening in the United States of America. Let us take an example of this system:

First you will have to find the time of sunrise for the day of the week you have chosen to work, and for the place you are living in. This information is often supplied in diaries, calendars, in occult magazines, and ephemerides. Most newspapers include this in the weather information. Let us take 2 January 1977. Sunrise on that day for the London area was 8:05 A.M. This means the 1st hour after sunrise is from 8:05-9:05 A.M., the second is from 9:05-10:05 A.M., the 9th hour after will be 4:05-5:05 P.M., the 18th hour is 1:05-2:05 A.M. (of the next day according to the first system), and so on. Let us take another example, this time 19 June 1977, for the London area once more. Sunrise this day is 3:42 A.M., but as British Summer Time (B.S.T.) is in operation in England during this period, all the clocks are one hour fast, or one hour in advance of Greenwich Mean Time (G.M.T.). This would make it 4:42 A.M. *by clock time*. So the first hour after sunrise would be 3:42-4:42 A.M. (4:42-5:42 A.M. by clock time), the 10th hour after sunrise would be 12:42-1:42 P.M. (1:42-2:42 P.M. by clock time), the 22nd hour will be 12:42-1:42 A.M. (1:42-2:42 A.M. by clock time, of the next day again, according to the first system given), and so on.

Let us take the hours of Mercury, once more using the 19 June 1977 example, when sunrise is 3:42 A.M. in London and B.S.T. is in operation. First his hours for the day that he rules – Wednesday – and then for the hours he sub-rules in our other example – Sunday. We will give the actual G.M.T. first, then in brackets the B.S.T. time with the hour added for *actual clock time* and the time you would use. On Wednesday he rules the 1st hour after sunrise, which would be 3:42-4:42 A M. (4:42-5:42 A.M.); the 8th hour, which is 10:42-11:42 A M. (11:42-12:42 P.M.); the 15th, which is 5:42-6:42 P.M. (6:42-7:42 P.M.); and finally the 22nd hour, which is 12:42-1:42 A.M. (1:42-2:42 a m.). Now, going back to the hours that he subrules on Sunday. He rules the 3rd hour after sunrise, which is at this time 5:42-6:42 A.M. (6:42-7:42 A.M.); the 10th hour, which is 12:42-1:42 P.M. (1:42-2:42 P.M.); the 17th hour, which is 7:42-8:42 P.M. (8:42-9:42 P.M.); and finally the 24th hour, which is 2:42-3:42 A.M. (3:42-4:42 A.M.) The same method is used for any particular planet you wish to work with. Now let us take a brief recap on the two methods you may use with this table.

In the first, which is the simpler, you use the column on the far right of the page. This gives the hours of the day as the face of a clock and this is how you use it. Having found the planet which rules the matter in which you have interest and also the day that he rules, you look down the column of that day for the planet. Every time you find it, you move along the line to the right-hand column, which will give you the hours he rules, and you use those times. You use the same procedure to find the hours the planet rules in the other days of the week.

If you choose the second system, then you ignore the times given on the far right, as you are going to work your own times out. To operate this system, you first obtain the time of sunrise for the locality in which you are living or where you are performing your ritual. Sixty minutes after that time is the 1st hour after sunrise, sixty minutes after that the 2nd, and so on throughout the remainder of the day. The warning about British Summer Time (for England, or any other system of Zone or Daylight Saving Times) must be taken into account which ever system you use, and the necessary adjustment made to clock times to bring it in line with Greenwich Mean Time. If you omit this, then you will be one hour out and working in the wrong time for the planet and angel required.

Let us take a look at some further considerations that may help to make this table more useful. This will also extend its use to the three modern or Extra-Saturnian planets of Uranus, Neptune, and Pluto. The following reflects my own personal methods of working with these planets. Like the members of any large family, some planets work better and more harmoniously with some planets than with others, with which they work badly, or at least reluctantly. It is not that they are 'enemies,' but that they simply operate in different ways. We ourselves cannot work well with people who use different methods from our own. If the feeling is very strong, we cannot work with them at all, though we may like them very much on a personal level. Sometimes the hours of the planets fall at inconvenient times for us. What can you do if the hours of the planets you wish to work with cannot be used? Can the hours of a friendly planet be used instead if it is more suitable? The answer is, Yes. It is still best, however, to use the correct hours, and the alternatives, though acceptable, should not be employed simply because you are too lazy to use the correct times. If you genuinely cannot use the correct times, then that is a different matter, but I stress the word 'genuinely.' Let us look at some of the alternatives.

Sun

The Sun works well with the hours of Mercury, Venus, Mars, and Jupiter. He is not too happy using the hours of Saturn and Uranus, though he can do in good aspect. Of dubious nature are the hours of Neptune and Pluto.

Moon

The Moon works well in the hours of Mercury, Venus, and Jupiter, with some reservations (good aspects) with the other water planet Neptune. Considered averse and to be avoided are the hours of Mars, Saturn, and Uranus, while the hours of Pluto are of a dubious nature. The Sun is variable according to aspect.

Mars

Mars works best with the hours of the Sun, a fire planet like himself, and with Jupiter's hours. Saturn's hours may be used if the other hours are not convenient. I personally would leave the hours of Uranus and Neptune.

Mercury

Mercury works well with the hours of the Sun, Venus, and Jupiter. He can be adverse in the hours of Mars, Saturn, and Uranus, so avoid these hours. The hours of Neptune and Pluto may also prove to be of a dubious nature.

Jupiter

Jupiter could use the hours of the Sun, Venus, and Neptune. I think I would avoid the hours of Mars, and definitely not use those of Saturn or Uranus, which are best avoided. I would not use any time connected with Pluto.

Venus

Venus works well in the hours of the Sun, Jupiter, and Neptune, but adversely in the hours of Uranus and Saturn. With Mars she is rather variable, depending on aspects at the time of the Ritual. The hours of Pluto are once more dubious.

Saturn

Saturn is really a law unto himself and tends to stand alone. Though he will work with others, I am not sure that he likes others to work with him, for he tends to be a bit of a 'loner.' Mars, however, could prove the exception to the rule, or when good aspects are being made to another planet, whose hours may be used if that planet is beneficial to the ritual – see note below.

Uranus

A difficult planet needing careful handling – another 'law unto himself.' He may find some affinity with the hours of Mars and Saturn. Try to avoid using any of the other planets unless well aspected.

Neptune

Will find affinity with the hours of Jupiter, Venus, and the Moon. I would leave the hours of the other planets alone if you can, unless well aspected.

Pluto

With the exception of the hours of Mars (the reason is given later), I would again try to leave the hours of the other planets alone, unless well-aspected.

N. B. Often a planet whose use is not recommended may be considered when it is making good aspects *at the time* of the ritual. For when planets are in good aspect they are, obviously, showing their 'helpful and positive' aspects, even those deemed 'bad planets' (who are not bad *all* the time). So, for example, if the ritual was of the planet Venus in a matter of love, the table advises *not* to use the hours of Saturn in this specific matter. If, however, Saturn was in good aspect to Venus at the time of the ritual (sextile or trine, not conjunct), then manifestly he is looking upon the matter benignly and could be used to some advantage, bringing as he may his positive gifts of stability, wisdom, and prudence. Thus, Saturn's hours could be used on this particular occasion if they are more convenient than those of Venus, or if the 'favours' he may grant are felt desirable. This example and practice may be extended to other planets in like fashion. Those unable to undertake astrological work should disregard these remarks and use the planetary combinations as suggested above, which will at least avoid making unintended errors.

Now, I can hear you say, quite rightly, 'Where are these hours of Uranus, Neptune, and Pluto?' These three planets were discovered much later than the time of the construction and use of the Table of Planetary Hours. The table is a very old one, constructed it is thought by Chaldean Astrologers on their system of astrology. When we come to how we may fit the new planets into the table so as to get constructive and effective results, we must move back into the realms of astrology, or at least its modern counterpart.

The Ancients used the seven planets given in the table and mentioned (in one way or another) in most ancient works, prebiblical and biblical, and in the works of many other nations. To these seven planets were assigned the twelve Signs of the Zodiac. The Sun only takes one – Leo, the Moon also has one, Cancer – while the remaining five planets take two signs each. Mercury – Gemini and Virgo; Venus – Taurus and Libra; Mars – Aries and Scorpio; Jupiter – Sagittarius and Pisces, and Saturn – Capricorn and Aquarius. With the discovery of the three new planets, Uranus (1781), Neptune (1846), and Pluto (1930), modern astrology caused three of the planets to surrender one of their signs to these new planets. Jupiter gave up his sign of Pisces to Neptune, Saturn gave up his sign of Aquarius to Uranus, and the last to be discovered, Pluto is usually conceded to the sign of Scorpio. So it follows that if these three new planets have taken over these signs from their original rulers, they may also use their hours and days, etc. So whenever use of these later planets is undertaken (see previous remarks), Uranus can use the hours of Saturn, Neptune the hours of Jupiter, and Pluto the hours of Mars. By the same token, this also applied to the days of the week you can use for their working: Saturn/Uranus using Saturday, Jupiter/Neptune using Thursday, and Mars/Pluto using Tuesday. Extensive use of this conjecture over quite a long period of time has not, as yet, proved it to be unacceptable or unworkable.

Table of Planetary Hours

AFTER SUNRISE	SUN.	MON.	TUES.	WED.	THUR.	FRI.	SAT.	FROM MIDNIGHT
1st	Sun	Moon	Mars	Mercury	Jupiter	Venus	Saturn	12-1 am
2nd	Venus	Saturn	Sun	Moon	Mars	Mercury	Jupiter	1-2 am
3rd	Mercury	Jupiter	Venus	Saturn	Sun	Moon	Mars	2-3 am
4th	Moon	Mars	Mercury	Jupiter	Venus	Saturn	Sun	3-4 am
5th	Saturn	Sun	Moon	Mars	Mercury	Jupiter	Venus	4-5 am
6th	Jupiter	Venus	Saturn	Sun	Moon	Mars	Mercury	5-6 am
7th	Mars	Mercury	Jupiter	Venus	Saturn	Sun	Moon	6-7 am
8th	Sun	Moon	Mars	Mercury	Jupiter	Venus	Saturn	7-8 am
9th	Venus	Saturn	Sun	Moon	Mars	Mercury	Jupiter	8-9 am
10th	Mercury	Jupiter	Venus	Saturn	Sun	Moon	Mars	9-10 am
11th	Moon	Mars	Mercury	Jupiter	Venus	Saturn	Sun	10-11 am
12th	Saturn	Sun	Moon	Mars	Mercury	Jupiter	Venus	-

AFTER SUNRISE	SUN.	MON.	TUES.	WED.	THURS.	FRI.	SAT.	FROM NOON
13th	Jupiter	Venus	Saturn	Sun	Moon	Mars	Mercury	12-1 pm
14th	Mars	Mercury	Jupiter	Venus	Saturn	Sun	Moon	1-2 pm
15th	Sun	Moon	Mars	Mercury	Jupiter	Venus	Saturn	2-3 pm
16th	Venus	Saturn	Sun	Moon	Mars	Mercury	Jupiter	3-4 pm
17th	Mercury	Jupiter	Venus	Saturn	Sun	Moon	Mars	4-5 pm
18th	Moon	Mars	Mercury	Jupiter	Venus	Saturn	Sun	5-6 pm
19th	Saturn	Sun	Moon	Mars	Mercury	Jupiter	Venus	6-7 pm
20th	Jupiter	Venus	Saturn	Sun	Moon	Mars	Mercury	7-8 pm
21st	Mars	Mercury	Jupiter	Venus	Saturn	Sun	Moon	8-9 pm
22nd	Sun	Moon	Mars	Mercury	Jupiter	Venus	Saturn	9-10 pm
23rd	Venus	Saturn	Sun	Moon	Mars	Mercury	Jupiter	10-11 pm
24th	Mercury	Jupiter	Venus	Saturn	Sun	Moon	Mars	11-12 am

Pronunciation Guide

Experience has shown that many beginners have a fear of mispronouncing occult terms, especially the Angelic Names. To assist those who feel this, here is a phonetic list to assist with the names of the angels. The stressed syllable is shown. Practise the sections first and then run them together.

MICHAEL or MIKAEL:	*My*-kel or Mick-*kay*-el.
GABRIEL:	*Gay*-bree-el (sometimes *Gab*-ree-el).
SAMAEL:	*Sam*-aye-el.
RAPHAEL:	*Raff*- aye el.
SACHIEL:	*Sa*-shay-el (short 'sa' – like sat without 't').
ANAEL:	*Anne*-aye-el.
CASSIEL:	*Cass*-see-el.
URIEL:	*Ooo*-ree-el.
ASARIEL:	Ass-*sar*-ree-el.
AZRAEL:	*Azz*-ree-el.

INDEX